Paul Dillon has been working in the area of drug education for the past 25 years. He trained as a primary school teacher in Western Australia and has since taught across all age groups, from pre-primary to high school students.

In the early 1990s he moved into the field of alcohol and other drugs, firstly working on community-based projects and education campaigns, and then becoming involved in a number of large research projects examining everything from ecstasy use to alcohol-related issues. Paul is best known for his media work, however, and continues to be regarded as a key social commentator in Australia. Appearing on a range of television programs including *Sunrise*, *TODAY* and *A Current Affair*, he is regularly asked to discuss topical issues, particularly in relation to young people and drugs. Paul had a regular spot on Triple J for seven years where he dealt with youth drug issues. He also hosted a popular Triple J website called 'Doing Drugs With Paul Dillon'.

Through his own business, Drug and Alcohol Research and Training Australia (DARTA), he is contracted by many agencies and organisations across the country to give regular updates on drug trends within the community. As a former school teacher, Paul has a passion for working with young people and continues to work with many school communities to ensure that they have access to good-quality information and best practice drug education.

Each year Paul presents information sessions on alcohol and other drugs to thousands of young people around the country. He is one of the few speakers in this area who is also privileged enough to speak to parents and the wider community, and his positive message about our young people continues to ensure that he is in great demand across Australia.

www.darta.net.au

TEENAGERS, ALCOHOL and DRUGS

PAUL DILLON

TEENAGERS, ALCOHOL, and DRUGS

What your kids really want and need to know about alcohol and drugs

ALLEN&UNWIN

First published in 2009

Copyright © Paul Dillon 2009

Allen & Unwin
83 Alexander Street
Crows Nest NSW 2065
Australia
Phone: (61 2) 8425 0100
Fax: (61 2) 9906 2218
Email: info@allenandunwin.com
Web: www.allenandunwin.com

National Library of Australia
Cataloguing-in-Publication entry:

Dillon, Paul, 1960–

Teenagers, alcohol and drugs : what your kids really want and need to know about alcohol and drugs / Paul Dillon

ISBN 978 1 74175 680 7 (pbk.)

Includes index.

Teenagers--Australia--Alcohol use
Teenagers--Australia--Drug use
Drug abuse--Australia--Prevention
Alcoholism--Australia--Prevention

362.290994

Index by Russell Brooks
Text design by Lisa White
Set in 11.5/15 pt Minion Pro by Bookhouse, Sydney
Printed and bound in Australia by Griffin Press

10 9 8 7 6 5 4 3 2 1

AUTHOR'S NOTE

The contents of this book are intended for information purposes only. The information contained in this book is not a substitute for, and is not intended to replace, independent professional legal or medical advice. Readers should consider the need to obtain any appropriate professional advice relevant to their own particular circumstances. Every effort has been made to ensure that the information is correct at the time of publication.

This book draws on a number of stories I have heard from young people and their parents over the years, but any information that might identify a particular person or event has been altered.

CONTENTS

PREFACE

My cousin David died from a heroin overdose in the first half of 2007. He was 34 years old. You often read about 'troubled' young people—that definitely described David. Red-haired and freckled, he had always been self-conscious and really didn't know where he fitted in the world. David had always had problems, but I also knew him to be a wonderful, caring human being.

I first got to know David in 2000; when my family discovered that he was using heroin, I flew to the UK to try to help him get onto some sort of drug treatment program. We clicked immediately. He was fascinated by my work in drug and alcohol education and was always asking me questions. Like most drug users he had no desire to hurt himself through his drug use and, although his behaviour could be extremely self-destructive, he was keen to find out as much as he could about different drugs and their effects.

Naturally, my aunt was devastated when she discovered David's heroin use. She came from a generation that simply did not understand illicit drug use. Although she had heard of heroin, it was something that characters in movies or television soap operas used—not her son. She had so many questions and didn't know where to go for the answers. She had done all the right things—she had gone to a counsellor, she had looked for a local parent support group—but she was confused and felt terribly alone.

David was a great success story in so many ways. Despite the occasional relapse, he found real happiness in the last year or two of his life. He had met a girl he really cared about, and his life appeared to be heading in the right direction. We will never really know what went wrong, but regardless of what happened I know he is in a better place.

His death has driven me to finally put pen to paper and write the book I have been thinking of writing for many years. This book is dedicated to David and his mother, my Aunty Pat, who were both looking for answers to a whole range of questions about drugs for a long time. Perhaps if they had had access to the information contained in the following pages things would have been different. I'm not saying for one minute that it would have prevented David experimenting with drugs, but it could have helped the parent–child relationship by providing them with some 'conversation starters'. The term 'generation gap' is one that is rarely used nowadays but in my experience it is alive and well when it comes to drugs. I hope with this book to bridge that chasm.

INTRODUCTION

Jana, Trish and Colette had been friends for many years. They were all sixteen and were halfway through their HSC. They enjoyed partying and although they were high achievers—Trish had topped her class the previous year—they made sure that they had a big night out at least once a fortnight. Colette was usually the one who organised the alcohol, as she had an older sister who would buy it for them. Their drink of choice was vodka.

On the night in question, the three girls were going to a party. They were picked up by Jana's boyfriend at Trish's house. Trish's parents were away for the weekend, though the parents of Colette and Jana didn't know this. The drinking had started before they left the house. 'Power drinking', or drinking as much as you could before you left home, was popular with their crowd. Jana also liked to drink through a straw, believing it would get her intoxicated faster. Although none of the girls necessarily liked the taste of vodka, they all drank it straight, and it wasn't long before they had polished off the first bottle. By the time they got to the party they were flying and out for a great night. However it soon became obvious that not all was going to plan.

Jana had started drinking before her friends and she had drunk substantially more. She began to feel extremely unwell and asked Colette and Trish to take her outside to be sick. The other two girls, who were also very intoxicated, helped Jana to the back garden, out of sight of the other partygoers. She vomited for some time but it was not until she began to slip in and out of consciousness that her friends became worried. They tried in vain to keep her awake until finally, in a state of panic, Trish went to find Jana's boyfriend and asked him to drive them back to Trish's house. By this time Jana was unable to walk and they had to carry her to the car.

The trip back was frightening. Her two friends kept giving Jana water to keep her hydrated, but she immediately threw it back up. She also wet herself and the smell of vomit and urine filled the car.

Although Jana's boyfriend wanted to stay, Trish and Colette decided to look after their friend alone. As soon as they got her into the house, they stripped her down to her underwear and carried her into the bathroom where they put her under a cold shower. She had now been unconscious for at least half an hour. When the cold water failed to revive her, and slapping her face didn't bring her around, Trish went to the kitchen and grabbed some slices of bread. Desperate to sober their friend up, the two girls force-fed Jana tiny pieces of bread, mistakenly believing that this would soak up the alcohol. Using their fingers to push the bread down her throat, Trish and Colette kept trying to bring their friend around until the girl's gag reflex kicked in and she threw up the bread they had been giving her. She coughed and spluttered and showed the first sign of life for some time.

Finally, the girls, who were now in tears, cleaned her up, took the still-unconscious Jana to the bedroom and put her to bed to let her sleep it off.

Thank goodness this story has a happy ending. Even though the girls did one of the most dangerous things you can do with a drunk, unconscious person—that is, put them to bed to 'sleep it off'—Jana survived.

This story was told to me by Trish and Colette after I had given a presentation at their school about young people and risk-taking.

The talks I give to teenagers in my role as a drug educator are full of anecdotes, stories I have been told by young people that I have met, incidents that I have been involved with over the years and, unfortunately, deaths I have heard about through my work. Trish and Colette shared their story with me after I told their class the risks associated with feeding bread to someone who is drunk. The girls were horrified to think that they could have endangered their friend's life.

'We thought we were doing the right thing. Why didn't anyone ever tell us that bread could be dangerous?' said Trish.

Why didn't anyone ever tell us? is the number one response I get from young people after I have given my presentation. It's a particularly difficult question to answer when it comes from a teenager who has just lost a friend as a result of alcohol or other drug use; when a girl they know has just died after drinking till she was unconscious and then choking on her own vomit; or when their best mate got so drunk he fell down on a road outside a party, hit his head and died from brain injuries; or when a classmate just drank so much that he passed out and never woke up.

There may be many reasons why we 'didn't ever tell them'. To begin with, there are many things they need or want to know that parents have never even thought to mention because they had no idea of the situations their children were facing. Have you ever discussed with your child how to look after someone who is vomiting after drinking alcohol? Would you even think of talking about the dangers of force-feeding bread to someone who is drunk in an attempt to sober them up?

We also need to take into account the fact that the lines of communication between parents and teenagers aren't always operating smoothly. Adolescence is a period of intense growth, not only physically but morally and intellectually, and it can be a time of great confusion and upheaval for many families. Teenagers are starting to separate from their parents and become more independent. At the same time, they are increasingly aware of how others, especially their peers, see them and they try desperately to fit in.

Accordingly, they may experiment with different looks and identities, which can result in conflict with parents.

It is important to remember that the primary goal of adolescence is to achieve independence. For this to occur, the young person will start to pull away from their parents, often the parent to whom they're closest. Parents may find that children who previously had been willing to conform to please them will suddenly begin asserting themselves strongly and rebelling against parental control.

As part of their maturing, young people start to think more abstractly and rationally. They're working out what they believe in—that is, their moral code—regarding a whole pile of issues, including alcohol and other drugs. Where drugs are concerned, things have changed a lot in the last twenty years. We know that those young people who do drink alcohol or use other drugs start using at an earlier age, they take a wider variety of substances, and they use more often. On top of this, there are a wider range of drugs available, and it seems that hardly a day goes by without the appearance of a media story reporting on some bizarre new substance threatening our children. These factors, among others, mean that today's youth face a wider range of potential problems than those in the past.

So what should we be doing about it? When it comes to helping parents with alcohol and other drug issues, educators and counsellors usually say things like 'talk to your kids' and 'keep the lines of communication open'. But these throwaway lines, although well meant, are really pretty useless unless you know what it is you're meant to talk about. What do you tell your children? What is it that they really want or need to know?

This book has been written as a conversation starter for parents. It includes many of the questions I have been asked over the years by both young people and their parents, and answers them as honestly as possible. We know that one of the best ways to deal with drug and alcohol issues is for families to have open and honest conversations so that each side can see what the other is concerned about when it comes to this controversial area. However, if that's not going to work for your family, read through the questions in the following pages and look at what young people want to know. What information are they really after? What is important to them at this stage in their lives?

When you examine the questions I have included from young people you will notice that many of them follow one theme: how can I keep myself and/or my friends as safe as possible? Despite some adults' negative perceptions about teens, they are often energetic, thoughtful and idealistic, with a deep interest in what's fair and right. In my experience, they also genuinely care about each other and want to look after themselves and their friends as best they can. At a time when our younger generation are getting a 'bad rap' from the media, it is important that we maintain some perspective. In actual fact we have a group of young people who are genuinely interested in collecting information that will help them to look after themselves and each other. Unfortunately, we are so obsessed with informing them about the negative side effects of drugs and alcohol (the information we think will deter them from using) that we are neglecting to give them the information they really want and need.

This book is all about helping families to be prepared. All any parents can really do is be there and do their best. There is no rule book when it comes to good parenting; every family is different and there are a whole range of different circumstances that will dictate how a parent responds to any problem that may arise. You can only do your best at the time—no one can expect you to do any more than that.

1
THE BASICS

When I'm addressing parent groups I usually start by asking the audience to think about where they get their information about drugs from. What has shaped their perception of the issue and how do they feel about drugs in relation to their own family?

Most parents know relatively little about alcohol and other drugs. They might have a bit of practical experience—usually in the form of vague memories from their teens or early twenties—but when it really comes down to it, most of the information they have has been obtained either through their friends or the media.

As I always say to young people, these are not the best sources of information. Friends don't mean to steer you in the wrong direction, but the sharing of information is going to subtly distort that information over time. You also need to remember that everyone has their own views on controversial issues such as drugs, and this can mean that when information is passed on, so too are the viewpoints, and this might affect the reliability of the information.

The media is no better. I have been working with the Australian media for over fifteen years now and I have seen first hand just how inaccurate many of the reports beamed into your home or presented in your daily newspaper are. Some media outlets have agendas, and in recent times we have seen some newspapers and television programs actually decide to take a stand on a particular issue or cause and attempt to change community viewpoints. This is not the appropriate place to debate the ethics of their actions, but it is important to remember that 'news' is often presented in a manner calculated to persuade you to think in a particular way.

Drug stories often appear under headlines designed to shock and horrify the readers, regardless of what the story is in fact trying to convey. I can't tell you how many times I have received an email or phone call from a responsible journalist to apologise for the appalling headline the editors have attached to an otherwise accurate story. Unfortunately, it is usually the headline that is remembered by the general public.

In this chapter, I will try to challenge some of the preconceived ideas you might have about alcohol and other drugs. Our views on issues such as drugs are formed based on a range of things, including our families and who we associate with, personal experiences and where we source our information. I hope that what you're about to read will make you critical of what you have been told in the past. If it does, go and read more, ask other people about their thoughts and beliefs in the area and learn to question the information you are provided with.

• Don't most young people experiment with alcohol and other drugs? Isn't it almost a rite of passage?

Last night I was watching TV and saw a new advertisement about young people and drug use. Over the top of an image of a group of young people was superimposed the words *One third of all young people have used an illegal drug.* That statistic sounds pretty scary for parents, and it is—there can be devastating consequences when anybody uses an illegal drug, and of course those risks are often greater for a young person. But why must we always be pushing out a negative message when it comes to this issue? Wouldn't it have been much more powerful and positive to present the same image with a statement saying that two thirds of young people *haven't* used an illegal drug?

No one should stick their head in the sand and pretend that there isn't a problem. When it comes to alcohol, it would be true to say that most young people will experiment with it at some time during their adolescence. However, the same cannot be said for illegal drugs, particularly when we're talking about teenagers. Most young people have never tried illegal drugs, they have no interest in these substances and they never will. Study after study confirms this, yet try to get this fact reported in the media and you hit a brick wall.

Interestingly, you often hit that very same brick wall when you speak to the teenagers themselves . . .

I had just finished my presentation at an inner-city high school by showing a slide revealing the number of young people who have *not* experimented with illicit drugs. This slide always raises eyebrows, with many teenagers surprised that the number is not significantly lower.

Max, a sixteen-year-old year eleven student and outspoken critical thinker, stood up to express his doubts.

'I find those figures very hard to believe,' he said. 'Everybody I know uses drugs. Where did you find those people who you surveyed?'

After explaining how the national survey data was collected I decided to challenge Max's statement.

'So everybody you know uses drugs?' I said. 'You're in a room with over 100 of your peers—are you saying that everyone in this room uses drugs?'

'No, of course not,' he replied. 'I don't mean people at school, I mean the people I know out of school. They all use drugs.'

I asked what drugs he was talking about and he informed me that cannabis was the drug of choice for 'everybody'.

'Give me a number,' I said. 'I want an actual number of people that you know for a fact use cannabis. I'm not talking about people you have heard about, or people you believe it of—tell me how many people you have seen smoking the drug.'

It took Max quite a while to respond and at first I thought my test was going to backfire, but he was an intelligent and thoughtful young man and was taking my request seriously. When he finally did give his answer it confirmed my belief that although he believed a considerable proportion of the people he knew (well, actually all of them) smoked cannabis, this was not the case.

'Five,' he said.

I love this story! I tell it at every school I go to and it always gets a great reception. Unfortunately, there is a perception out there, even among young people, that most people have used drugs. But when you take a few moments to challenge that perception you can get some really interesting results. I will often get young people coming up to me after I tell the story about Max saying that when they really questioned it they realised they didn't know as many people who used drugs as they thought they did.

There are two words I really dislike that we tend to overuse when talking about alcohol and drugs—'all' and 'everybody'. If you take a couple of minutes to think about it, you'll realise that statements like 'everybody does it' and 'all teenagers go through that stage' just don't add up. 'Everybody' doesn't do it and not 'all' teenagers go through that stage—these generalisations need to be challenged and, unfortunately, we don't do that enough.

For some reason young people really feed into this mythology and are their own worst enemies when it comes to reinforcing stereotypes about teenagers and drug use. When I work with large groups of teenagers I often start off a discussion by asking them what they know about drugs. Inevitably, the first few statements from the floor tend to be along the lines of:

- Drugs are everywhere.
- Everyone takes drugs.
- Peer pressure makes it really difficult for teenagers to resist drugs and alcohol.
- Everyone I know gets drunk.

It's interesting to note that this is the response you get from the large group but when you talk to them in smaller numbers you quickly find that these sweeping generalisations don't hold up. Questions like 'Do you or your best friend use drugs?' or 'When was the last time you saw someone use an illegal drug?' are often answered with 'No' and 'Never'.

Many of you would have seen current affairs shows where they get a group of young people together and ask them questions about the drug problem. The interviewer usually asks them exactly the same type of questions as I do in a group discussion, and the young people respond with the generalisations I have listed above, reinforcing the belief that most, if not all, teenagers are regularly using illegal drugs and getting drunk all the time.

On one of my school visits I met a particularly amazing group of kids. These articulate, intelligent year eleven students spoke candidly about their lives, questioned and were critical of the data given in the presentation, and really took advantage of a lively discussion session at the end of the talk.

It so happened that the following week one of the current affairs shows contacted me and asked me to assist them in pulling together a group of young people for a forum on drugs. I immediately knew which school I was going to approach. This was a group that I could trust to be honest and open with their answers, and to avoid falling into the trap of speaking in stereotypes. I contacted the school and the interview was arranged.

On the day of filming, prior to the arrival of the interviewer and camera crew, I had a meeting with those students who had been selected by the school and given permission by their parents to participate. I sat them down and ran through the type of questions I thought would be asked.

'How big a problem is drugs for teenagers?' was my first question.

'Of course it's an issue. There are some kids in our year who have used drugs but they're in the minority,' was the first of many responses the group gave. 'Alcohol is the biggest problem, but even then most of us only drink at parties and, although some people can get pretty wasted, the majority drink pretty sensibly.'

And it went on like that. The answers were spontaneous: I didn't brief them, I didn't try to encourage them to respond in a particular way.

The camera crew arrived, and the presenter introduced herself to the group and explained how the forum would work. She would ask a series of questions and then she wanted them to speak freely and honestly about their experiences and thoughts on the issue. The whole idea was for them to bounce off one another and for the conversation to flow. I was excited—this was going to be great!

The camera started to roll and the first question was much the same as the one I had asked the group only half an hour before: 'So what can you tell me about young people and drugs—is it a problem?'

I have no idea what happened, but somehow that group of articulate and intelligent teenagers turned into the children from *Village of the Damned* as soon as the camera started rolling. Their eyes glazed over and out came the stereotypical generalisations. 'Drugs are everywhere', 'Everyone does drugs'—the clichés just kept coming. And of course, the interviewer lapped them all up; it was perfect television.

In my experience, kids often tell us what they think we want to hear. Now no parent will tell you that they want to hear that young people take drugs or drink to excess—but it is what many people believe because that is what they have been fed by the media and society in general. Young people pick up on this very quickly, and rehash these messages, even if it is not their own experience.

Let's not forget that not all young people are the same, and this is particularly true when it comes to attitudes and values around drugs. Even when it comes to alcohol use, young people are not one homogenous group. When I talk to groups of teenagers I usually divide them into three key categories, two of which we rarely acknowledge. The first is the loudest and the most obvious: those young people who drink to excess. There is much debate as to whether this group is growing—I don't believe it is, although it is quite clear that heavy-drinking teenagers are consuming at much riskier levels and at a younger age.

The next group comprises the ones who drink responsibly. They don't drink regularly and when they do they usually consume a small amount. This does not mean there are no risks involved in their drinking behaviour, but we do need to acknowledge that these young people are trying to do 'the right thing'.

Finally we have the abstainers. An interesting fact, rarely discussed, is that 20–25 per cent of Australian school-based sixteen- and seventeen-year-olds describe themselves as non-drinkers. We never speak about these young people and their decision; in fact, we completely ignore them, making them feel even more alienated from their peer group than they do already.

We need to acknowledge that many young people will drink alcohol at some time during their adolescence and some may experiment with one or more illegal drugs. As a parent, you need to let your child know where you stand in regard to alcohol and drinking behaviour, and the use of illegal drugs. Letting your teenager know how you feel about sensitive topics, and explaining your viewpoints clearly and without passing judgment, is not only going to assist them to develop positive values but will also strengthen your relationship with your child.

• When is the right time to start talking to my kids about drugs?

I'm a firm believer that you should start talking about drugs the minute you start giving them to your child. We live in a world where pharmaceutical companies have been able to convince us that for every problem we have, there is a drug that can fix it. If you are depressed, you take a pill. If you have a headache, you take a pill. We start medicating our children from a very early age, training them to be very effective drug users.

Whether the drugs are medicinal, legal or illegal, our children should be informed about the risks associated with drug use. When it comes to pharmaceutical drugs or over-the-counter medications, children need to be made aware of the importance of appropriate use. In the first few years of primary school, drug education lessons focus on this area and do it extremely well. They don't talk about drugs being 'bad', instead they discuss the idea that drugs can help people when used appropriately, and it is the *misuse* of drugs that can cause problems.

Unfortunately, many parents don't bother to talk to their children about medicines, seemingly forgetting that they are drugs too. These days, it is rare to get a doctor's appointment that lasts longer than ten minutes. No sooner are we escorted into a doctor's surgery to explain what is wrong with us than we are handed a prescription and ushered out. There's no time to ask what it is we are taking and, even though pharmacists will often give us some basic instructions to accompany the drugs we are given, because it has been prescribed by a doctor we don't even question how safe or how dangerous it might be. We simply take it—no questions asked.

Over-the-counter medications are used in the same way. The last time your child complained of a headache or a pain, what was the first thing you said to them? I can almost guarantee that you told them to go and take a pill of some description. I bet you didn't ask them why they had a headache or suggest a non-pharmaceutical option—you most likely went for the quick fix. Using a drug to solve a problem has become second nature.

Let's get down to brass tacks here—most drugs can be used in a positive way. Heroin is an extremely effective painkiller, cannabis can ease the symptoms of a number of medical conditions, and there is even some evidence that ecstasy (MDMA) can be useful in the treatment of post-traumatic stress disorder. This is not to say that these drugs are safe and that there are safe ways to use them. All drugs have a degree of risk associated with their use and we need to make that perfectly clear to our children. If we can communicate these risks to them about legally available products, such as drugs we obtain from a doctor or headache tablets we get from the supermarket, we have a much better chance of conveying effective messages about illegal drugs.

With very young children, I suggest you start by reading aloud the directions contained on a medication's packaging when you administer it. This sends a simple message to your child about the importance of following instructions when it comes to medications. You need to explain to your child that these directions are vital, as medicines can be extremely dangerous when used inappropriately.

Unfortunately, many parents only decide to talk to their child about drugs when a crisis situation occurs. This 'crisis' can be as serious as finding out that their child is actually using drugs or as mundane as their child being invited to a teenage party for the first time. Trying to have a discussion about drug use at a time like this is unlikely to be a positive experience for either you or your child. Your teenager will feel uncomfortable at best, and threatened at worst, by having the issue raised at this time. As a result, you are likely to feel frustrated and angry at their response, leading to greater friction and a breakdown in the parent–child relationship.

Remember that it is impossible for any relationship to exist without positive communication. When it comes to talking about any difficult subject, and that includes alcohol and other drugs, don't think of it as a five-minute 'talk'—it's about building an ongoing dialogue. Of course, there will need to be an opening conversation and that can be difficult, but once you've broken the ice it will get easier. As your children grow up, they will need more and more information, so start early and build on the conversation as your teenager matures.

There are lots of opportunities for parents to introduce the issue of alcohol and other drugs to their children. Rather than setting aside a specific time in the day to sit down with your child and raise the topic, thus making the whole experience like a school lesson, parents should look for opportunities in everyday life to talk about drugs. No parent need look any further than the evening news for these opportunities.

Over the past few years, many drug-related stories have received huge coverage. The Schapelle Corby story and the plight of the 'Bali Nine' in particular have captured the attention of most Australians, regardless of their age.

At the height of the Schapelle Corby case I was receiving many calls from primary school teachers who wanted some advice on how to handle the issue. Their young students were asking questions about the story and raising the issue of cannabis. What was cannabis? What did it do? Why was this woman going to jail for taking the drug into Bali? The teachers were worried about the potential risks involved with talking about a drug like cannabis in a classroom setting, particularly with very young students. At parent sessions I was running I was finding that parents were feeling exactly the same way. Their children were full of questions they didn't know how to answer.

As tragic as these stories are, they provide perfect opportunities for a parent to raise the issue of drug use and the associated risks. Your children are going to learn an awful lot about your attitudes and beliefs towards alcohol and drug use from what you say in response to news stories like these.

I am not suggesting that you sit down with your young child and watch the news together. The nightly news program with its stories about death and destruction—whether they deal with natural disasters, terrorist activity or war—can be incredibly traumatising for most young people. That said, many of these stories are brought up in casual conversation at home, or kids overhear discussions between adults or older siblings, or these topics might arise in the classroom or in the playground. As much as you might want to shield your child from these sorts of stories, you are essentially fighting a losing battle.

Talk to your children as early and as often as possible. Make sure you speak to them about the range of drugs available, with an emphasis on those that they are most likely to come into contact with at their particular stage of development. For the very young, including primary school-aged children, most of the conversations you'll have will centre around prescription or over-the-counter medications. It may also be useful at this time to talk to them about how *you* use drugs, whether they be drugs prescribed by a doctor or alcohol and tobacco.

Don't wait for a crisis to occur to start the conversation, and try to avoid turning the discussion into a lecture.

> Stuart is a health education teacher with two nephews who would frequently visit their favourite uncle.
>
> After a long day of outdoor activities they would usually watch a movie. The boys could choose the film, within reason, and without fail they would select some American comedy that their uncle would hate! It didn't take long for Stuart to notice that some of the material in these movies went against everything he knew was best practice when it came to drug use. Not only did they normalise drug use but the writers often employed drug use (mostly cannabis) to elicit a laugh, and rarely did they discuss the negative consequences of use.
>
> In an effort to correct the message the movies were sending, Stuart decided to use the movies as an educational tool. When something came up in the film that he felt was inappropriate, he would stop the film and discuss it with his nephews, almost using it as a classroom activity.
>
> As you can imagine, it wasn't long before the boys didn't want to watch movies with Uncle Stuart anymore!

The best of intentions can lead to negative outcomes if they are not well thought through. Stuart's experience with his nephews provides a valuable lesson on how not to raise the issue of drugs with young people. Turning opportunities for conversations into school lessons is going to be met with a great deal of resentment and the kids will simply tune out.

You should never push the subject. If your child makes it clear that he or she doesn't want to discuss an issue with you at that particular time and there is not a crisis that has to be dealt with, respect their wishes and try again later. Let them know that you are willing to talk about the subject and that you are always available should they need information or help.

• Do shock tactics work? Will trying to scare my kids put them off experimenting with drugs?

When Prince Harry was much younger and he admitted to getting drunk and experimenting with cannabis it received a great deal of media coverage. Also receiving attention was his father's response: that he might take his son to a rehabilitation centre to talk to 'addicts' in an attempt to make him see the error of his ways.

So what do we know about the effectiveness of such 'shock tactics'? Those who have had little to do with drugs often regard it as the right thing to do. The drug users tell their personal stories of how drugs ruined their lives and as a result the listener will be put off drugs. Many involved with the drug culture see this response as a waste of time, though, believing that shock tactics like these rarely have an impact on a young person who is enjoying the effects of their drug of choice.

Shock tactics encompass a variety of different techniques. Many of you will remember a police officer coming to your school and showing you pictures of terrible car accidents in an effort to prevent speeding and/or drink-driving. Photographs of diseased lungs and other body parts are often used in health lessons to dissuade young people from smoking.

Yes, these images shock and horrify—but do they really stop young people from partaking in risk-taking behaviour?

Most people, particularly young people, believe that 'it is never going to happen to me'. No matter what you tell them, no matter how good the information is, no matter how shocking the image, their behaviour will not change unless something happens to them directly.

Shock tactics have a place in public health education. They may prevent some people from taking part in risky behaviour. However, it is impossible to establish how many of those people would have become involved in that activity in the first place!

• How can I reduce the influence of peer pressure?

I was asked to present a short talk to a group of year six students on the far north coast of New South Wales. It is unusual for me to present to such a young group of people but the teachers involved convinced me that it was appropriate. Before I began the actual talk I asked the students what they knew about drugs . . . Could they name some drugs that they had heard of? No real surprises there—the hands went up and we got a whole range of responses, including alcohol, tobacco, drugs from a doctor, cannabis, paracetamol, ecstasy and heroin. Then I asked them *why* people used drugs. With that, every hand went up in the air at the same time, and when I asked them for their answer the whole class responded in unison: 'Peer pressure.'

This was a group of eleven- and twelve-year-olds and I was surprised by the certainty of their response, so I asked them to explain what they meant. What was 'peer pressure'? My question was met with a deafening silence—not one of the students could give me an answer.

Like so many others around the country these students had heard the term 'peer pressure' regularly; in fact, they had most probably had it pushed down their throats for quite some time, and they had bought into it without having any real idea what it meant. Unfortunately, many Australian parents are in the same position.

Some parents seem to love the concept of peer pressure. It's a great way of shifting responsibility for certain behaviours off their own child with the excuse that 'someone else made them do it'.

No parent wants to acknowledge fault in their child, particularly if other people have identified the problem. The concept of peer pressure allows parents an 'out' when it comes to their child's negative behaviour. When you think of peer pressure, images come to mind of one child pushing another into taking part in some activity that he or she may not really want to do. In my experience this does not usually happen; most young people do not put pressure on others to use illegal drugs. In fact, you often find the reverse is true.

> Malcolm had been using ecstasy for over eight years when I spoke to him. He had first used the drug when he was twenty years old after associating with a group of clubbers for almost twelve months. He had observed his group of friends using ecstasy and had decided to try it. When he asked his friends to provide the drug the response he got was not exactly the one he was expecting. They asked him whether he was aware of the risks and if he was really sure that he wanted to start using ecstasy. Malcolm was confused and surprised by the response and for a while viewed his friends as hypocritical. However, he quickly realised that they were trying to look after him and make sure that he truly did know what he was getting into.

Although this story challenges a lot of what people believe about peer pressure, the truth is that most young people do not 'push' their friends into doing something they don't want to do.

Of course, we should never underestimate the impact that peer pressure can have on our children, particularly when it comes to alcohol, but far more important at this time is 'social pressure' or influence. This is something that we rarely talk about, but it is far more likely to affect teenagers' behaviour as it is much more subtle and, because it is everywhere and all-pervasive, far more difficult to control.

What made Malcolm want to start using ecstasy? According to Malcolm what had influenced his decision was not pressure from his friends but what he had observed: the people he had been partying with were having a 'good time' on ecstasy. Although there had been 'peer influence', it was much more an overall 'social influence' that led to his desire to try the drug.

This social pressure comes in many forms. It can take the form of advertising, be found on television and in movies, or arise from observing celebrities and their behaviour. Once again I need to emphasise that I'm not saying that peers don't play a part—but always remember that there are many other influences at work.

At one time or another we all need assistance dealing with social pressure. Even as adults we occasionally ask people to help us in this area. Have you ever had a friend call you on your mobile to help get you out of a social situation? In fact, a great many parents actually use their children as an excuse: 'I'd love to but I've got to pick up the kids' or 'That sounds great but we've got the kids' sport on Saturday morning'.

Teenagers sometimes need these 'outs' as well, particularly when dealing with social pressure. The adolescent years are all about learning where you fit in the world, and young people quickly work out what will get you accepted within a peer group and what will find you out on your ear. Going to parties and drinking alcohol is part of what some teenagers do every weekend, and those young people who decide that it is not for them often have to suffer the consequences.

Travelling around the country over the years I have met many young people who have developed strategies to deal with this. Some of these strategies are extremely sophisticated and show a wisdom way beyond their years. Possibly the most impressive is illustrated by the following story, which not only provided an out for some boys who were sick and tired of getting drunk every weekend, but also contributed to the reduction of alcohol-related problems in their town, according to the local police.

In a small country town in central New South Wales I met four young men who had decided to change their drinking behaviour.

The town they lived in had a range of alcohol problems, including—though not limited to—teenage binge drinking.

By the age of sixteen, these youths had been drinking for the past twelve to eighteen months. Their weekends comprised of drinking with a few friends on Friday nights, playing football on Saturday afternoons, followed by a major party or gathering on Saturday night. There was little else to do in this very small town and the social pressure to 'fit in' and 'be one of the boys' made it extremely difficult for any of them to break away from this routine, even though they all found they weren't enjoying going out and getting wrecked every weekend the way they once did.

Finally, one of them came up with the idea of asking the coach of their football team whether he would consider changing one of the training sessions from an evening mid-week to midmorning on Sunday. That way the boys could still go out on Saturday night but they would now have an excuse not to stay out all night and drink to excess.

When they put their suggestion to the coach (without revealing the real reason behind the idea) he was initially reluctant, worried that Sunday trainings would not be well attended and also concerned about the impact on his own social life. But he agreed to put the proposal to the rest of the team and, if there was unanimous agreement, he would consider the idea.

To his surprise the proposal was supported by all team members! Footy training is now held on Sunday morning and, according to the community, this has had a positive impact on alcohol-related problems as far as young males are concerned. The boys can still party but if they want to finish up early or moderate their alcohol consumption they save face—all due to a little lateral thinking by four young men.

This was, as I said, a fairly sophisticated strategy. For the most part, the strategies that adolescents develop to help them in this area are fairly simple and straightforward. Here are the top ten 'outs' that I have collected from teenagers over the years. Not all of them are great, but they cover a range of different ways of saying 'no', including excuses (often using information they have picked up in drug education lessons at school) and delaying or putting off the situation.

- 'I am allergic to alcohol.'
- 'The medication I'm on at the moment doesn't mix well with alcohol.'
- 'I'd love to smoke but I have an uncle with a mental health problem.' (A very popular one for getting out of smoking cannabis.)
- 'I got really drunk last week and I'm trying to have a few weeks off.'
- 'Dad found out I was drinking last weekend and I'll be grounded if I get caught again.'
- 'We've got a big game next week and I want to be as fit as possible.'
- 'Mum's picking me up this evening and she always checks my breath when I get in the car.'
- 'Maybe later—I've already had a few and I just want a break for a while.'
- 'My uncle is a police officer and he is staying at our house tonight. I've got to be really careful.'
- 'Dad's an alcoholic and we've been told it could run in the family.' (Not a great one for you, Dad, particularly if you don't have an alcohol problem, but if it works for them . . .)

Of course, not all teenagers need an out—some young people are strong and confident enough to simply say no—but many young people do need help in this area, and it is important that they have some other strategy in place to assist them when they find themselves in difficult situations. Even though school-based drug education gives young people the opportunity to discuss and develop such skills and strategies, a parent who has a good relationship with his or her child may be able to do it far more effectively.

You may have noticed that out of the ten statements listed, five of them involve a relative of some sort (obviously your children have been watching the excuses you use for different things!). It would appear that many young people are using their parents as an excuse in some instances, so it makes great sense to sit down and ask them if you can help them with this in some way. Not all teenagers are going to respond positively to this conversation, although many parents are surprised at the reaction they do receive when they offer assistance.

It can be hard to find the right time to approach your child; make sure it's an occasion when you and your teenager are alone and there is no likelihood of an interruption. (Conversations in the car can be very positive—they can't get away and they don't have to look at you!) Ask your child if they have ever been in a situation with their friends which they found difficult or uncomfortable. You could use a story from this book as an example. Talk about peer and social pressure and maybe discuss some of the things that you do to help you through difficult situations. Offer them your help in coming up with practical strategies to assist them in these situations. If now is not the 'right time', let them know that they can come to you at any time and you will try to help them. Working together to come up with an 'out' strategy has worked for many parents and their teenage children.

Anita and her daughter Halle had a code word that they devised when Halle was fifteen. This word was to be used by Halle in either a text message, a phone call or a conversation whenever she wanted to be taken out of a situation. For example, if Halle was at a party and she wanted to come home but didn't feel confident enough to tell her friends she wanted to leave of her own accord, she would simply text her mother a message which contained the code word. Anita would wait a few minutes and then call her daughter to say there was an emergency and that she would need to pick her up straightaway. Anita was made out to be the 'bad guy' and Halle retained her place in her social group.

This sort of strategy works extremely well in families with great communication and trust. It has to be used sparingly, though; young people are not stupid and if Halle overused the code word her friends would soon realise what was going on.

So far I have talked more about dodging peer pressure than reducing its impact. But there are a number of ways in which parents can lessen the effect of peer influence. Possibly one of the most important is for parents to correct the common teenage misperception that 'all teenagers drink lots of alcohol'. This false belief leads some teenagers to feel they need to drink to excess in order to fit in with their peers. The truth is, although most teenagers have tried alcohol, only a small (but very visible) proportion drink alcohol to get drunk. It is important to provide your teenagers with objective information to prevent them from falling into this trap. For example, a media story that recently received a great deal of publicity around the country focused on the fact that 'one out of ten Australian teenagers are binge drinkers'—that means that nine out of ten aren't! Make your child aware of the fact that if he or she drinks alcohol responsibly or chooses not to drink then he or she is in the majority.

Parents need to remember that their child's peer group only becomes really powerful when the parent–adolescent relationship is breaking down. Maintaining a positive relationship with your child during this difficult time called adolescence is imperative. This doesn't mean that you can't say 'no' and that you don't set rules and boundaries—in fact, you should be doing just that. But if parents can maintain a positive, caring and open relationship with their child they will be in a good position to play a major part in decisions young people make about alcohol and other drugs—and even appear to have a greater influence than their kids' peer groups in many cases. Listen and talk to your children at every opportunity, become involved in their lives and believe in the power of your family—you can make a difference!

• Does the area I live in determine the drug my child may experiment with?

One of the most popular requests I get from journalists around the country is for statistics on drug use for a specific area. Country or community newspaper reporters are always particularly interested in knowing how many people in their area use one type of drug or another. They are always staggered to find out that those statistics are not available. This does not mean that the figures do not exist, it is just that they are not always made available to the general public.

In Australia we know a great deal about the prevalence of drug use, particularly when compared to other countries. We have a number of very large surveys that are conducted fairly regularly and this gives us a pretty good idea about what is going on. We also live in a country where, for the most part, people do not fear being honest about reporting their drug use in a confidential survey. This would not necessarily be the case in many other parts of the world. The information we have is not perfect and the figures are often misused by people, but we are able to identify trends and see if there are any emerging problems that need to be dealt with.

The statistics are often broken down into state and territory figures, but you rarely see them broken down into any more detail than that. There are several reasons for this, but primarily it has to do with the fact that the more detail that is given, the greater the chance of being able to identify who provided the information. This is especially true of the survey that examines secondary school students' drug use.

Even though we don't have the necessary statistics, we do have enough information available to suggest that there are certain areas around the country that are more likely to have particular problems than others. For parents, this means that the area you live in could help determine the drugs your child may come into contact with.

There are three factors that are of great importance if someone is going to choose to take a drug, whether that drug is legal, illegal or pharmaceutical. To some extent, all of these may be influenced by the area in which you live. These factors are:

- availability
- cost
- cultural acceptance of drug use by the peer group.

Obviously there are some areas where there is a greater availability of some drugs than in others. Cannabis is possibly the best example of this, although possible ecstasy use was once heavily influenced by where you lived.

The far north coast of New South Wales is acknowledged as an area where cannabis is widely available for a variety of reasons, including the fact that there is a great deal of cannabis grown there. For many years ecstasy use was far less likely to occur in country areas, particularly inland regional centres, due to the drug being less readily available in those areas when compared to the cities and suburbs. Ecstasy use was also linked closely to the nightclub and dance scene, something strongly associated with the inner city; as the dance scene has expanded, however, many regional areas have also seen ecstasy use rise.

Even in areas where certain drugs are more available, they are not falling out of the sky! You still need to know someone who can get them for you. As much as the media would love to tell you that there are evil drug dealers hanging out at the end of the schoolyard, this is not the case, and illicit drugs are not that easy to come by.

One thing that many people forget is that drugs are expensive. In fact, Australia has some of the most expensive drugs in the world. It is true that some drugs are now much cheaper than they used to be, particularly ecstasy, which has dropped from an average of $60 per pill to $35 over a ten-year period, but is still much more expensive than in places such as the UK, where a pill can cost as little as £1 ($2.50). Nonetheless, illicit drugs are usually way out of the price range for most young people. It is not until they hit their twenties and have a job and a disposable income that they can afford to outlay a sizeable proportion of their wages on drugs. We don't talk about it enough, but money is one of the major barriers to young people experimenting with alcohol and other drugs.

This is why I'm always surprised when I hear of parents handing out large sums of money to their teenage children. It is among this group of young people that I tend to see the most risky behaviour when it comes to alcohol and several other drugs, particularly ecstasy. It is usually the affluent areas where you tend to see a wider range of illicit drug use occurring among teenagers because—to put it bluntly—they have the money. I can pretty well guarantee that you will not find groups of young people in lower socioeconomic areas downing bottles of vodka and whisky on a regular basis. They simply don't have the money to cover the cost. Now that's not to say that there are not alcohol or other drug problems in these areas—it's just that they're different problems. These young people are going to be looking for cheaper alcohol products with the highest alcohol content to ensure intoxication. As far as other drugs are concerned, if they can afford to buy anything they are going to be looking for a substance which gives them the 'biggest bang for their buck'.

The final thing to consider is the cultural acceptance of drug use by the peer group. Some peer groups have a greater acceptance of drug use than others, with some frowning on the use of one particular drug while encouraging the use of another. Of course, there are also peer groups that do not find drug use of any kind acceptable.

If you live on the coast there is every likelihood that the surf culture may play a part in your child's life. The surf culture has been around for a long time and has an acknowledged drug culture associated with it. Cannabis use, in particular, is closely linked to the surfer scene, and if your child becomes a part of this group then it is vital that you discuss how you feel about the drug and its use with him or her. Not all young people involved in surf culture will use cannabis but it is highly likely that they will come into contact with the drug at one time or another.

Glenn is the father of two teenage boys, both heavily involved in the surf scene. He was a surfer himself and is well aware of the drug culture that existed back when he was an adolescent and still exists today.

'I've found myself stuck between a rock and a hard place when it comes to talking to my boys,' he told me. 'I dabbled in dope when I was young but only a couple of times. I wish I hadn't! I didn't enjoy it and now I can't turn around and honestly say to my boys that I didn't smoke the stuff!

'I've been as honest as I could and followed the advice of a friend who told me to focus on why I stopped smoking. Quite honestly I never got anything out of it and I saw one of my mates end up with a mental health problem. Since that time he has never worked a day. Both my boys know him and see him as a bit of a loser, which can't be a bad thing.

'I don't kid myself that one or both of them won't try the drug. They do know that I don't want them to and that if I find out they have there will be consequences. It's going to be tough for them though—the surf culture has always had a bong and some dope attached somewhere.'

The same is true of the dance scene. If you live in the inner suburbs of any major city around the country, or in a regional university centre, there is every chance your son or daughter may attach themselves to this scene. Historically there is a strong link between ecstasy and the dance culture. The drug's popularity has increased internationally as the dance scene has grown around the world. Some people who attend dance events and nightclubs use ecstasy, as well as other drugs, to alter their perception and enhance the experience. Whether or not a young person involved in the dance scene decides to use drugs or not, parents need to know that it is highly likely that their children will come into contact with drugs if they regularly attend dance events. As a result it is important to talk about drugs like ecstasy whenever possible. Even though you may not know much about them, take the opportunity to learn about them with your child.

Young people who are part of one of these cultural groups also need to know the legal consequences of taking illegal drugs. New policing strategies such as drug detection dogs and roadside drug testing have resulted in more young people from some of these groups being prosecuted for drug offences. Let your child know how being caught using drugs will affect the rest of their life.

As much as you may be tempted (for all the right reasons, I'm sure), trying to prevent your child from being part of a group that he or she has chosen is likely to cause a great deal of problems in your relationship. It is important for parents to voice their concerns and set rules and boundaries around behaviour. Let your child know what the consequences will be if these rules are broken and follow through with these. If you are concerned about drug use, let them know and tell them why you are worried. Keep the lines of communication open and let them know at every opportunity that they can come to you and talk about anything at any time.

Finally, make it very clear where you stand on the use of illegal drugs. As much as you may believe your views do not matter to your child, research shows that parental influence is still a major factor in the decisions many young people make.

The area in which you live may make a difference to the drug your child comes into contact with. It is the relationship you have with your child, however, that is more likely to have a greater influence on how your child responds to that contact and the decision to experiment with that drug or not.

• Where do young people get drugs from?

One of the classic drug stereotypes is that of the evil drug dealer or 'pusher' lurking in the shadows of the schoolyard trying to entice children with his wares. This image plays into all the fears that parents have about drugs and how they are distributed. It reinforces the belief that young people have drugs pushed onto them by unscrupulous people who try to get them 'addicted' to a substance so that they can continue to make money from their clients' misery.

Television and movies have cemented the belief in many people's minds that drugs are usually purchased 'on the street'. Without question there are some street drug markets that exist in Australia, with Kings Cross in Sydney being the most well known, but they are few and far between. Those who use these street markets are usually entrenched drug users, most often injectors, who have a range of other social problems. It would be extremely unusual to find young people who are considering experimenting with drugs utilising street dealers.

One of the great myths about young people and drugs is that they have drugs 'pushed' onto them. The truth is, some adolescents actually hunt them out. Their interest has been sparked by what they have seen in their friendship group, on television or in the movies, and they want to see what all the fuss is about. In reality, most young people obtain drugs through friends. Friends who can provide access to drugs are regarded as valuable assets. Young people who supply drugs to their friends would never regard themselves as 'dealers'; most of them see themselves as simply providing a 'service'. Their friends want drugs and they are able to provide them.

This has been clearly illustrated in many of the ecstasy-related deaths that have occurred over the years when the person who sold the pills to the deceased is identified and prosecuted. Often these suppliers were friends of the young person who has died and in some cases they actually handed themselves in after the death because of their feelings of guilt.

On the information we have, it would seem that very few of these young suppliers make significant amounts of money from selling drugs to friends. There's no denying that illicit drugs are definitely big business and there are a lot of people who make very large amounts of money from dealing and supplying, but, contrary to popular belief, selling small quantities to friends is not a big money-spinner.

So if it's not about the money, why do some young people take these enormous risks? The limited information we have about this type of supplying among friendship groups seems to suggest that most of the young people who are involved in the supply of drugs do so to supplement their own drug use.

Natalie couldn't really remember the first time she supplied drugs to a friend. When I asked her whether she considered herself a dealer she was horrified. She was twenty years old and had been part of the dance scene for the past couple of years. She knew one or two people who sold ecstasy and when one of her good friends approached her to ask if Natalie could find her some pills, she didn't hesitate to make the call and become the link between the supplier and her friend.

Things had got a little out of hand since that time and she admitted that now not a week went past when she did not provide drugs to someone. The number of pills that were changing hands had grown exponentially and she now had a name as someone who could get you drugs. Natalie had never made money from selling drugs, however each of her suppliers (and she now had at least four) gave her a free pill for every ten that she sold.

She had contacted me because she'd just found out that one of her suppliers had been arrested. Only a couple of months before this one of her best friends had been jailed for four years for the supply of drugs. Natalie started to feel the world around her crumbling and didn't know what to do or who to talk to. What seemed like an innocent act of 'helping a friend out' in the first place had somehow changed into her becoming a drug dealer, with the very real possibility of a jail term if she were caught. She just couldn't work out how it had happened.

Of course there are always those young people who make foolish decisions, like selling drugs to be accepted by their peer group. As

I've said, among certain groups, the person who is able to supply drugs is regarded as a valuable asset. You can become pretty popular if you're able to provide good-quality drugs at a reasonable price.

Adolescence is such a difficult time for some young people, and they have such a great need to be accepted by those around them, that unfortunately some of them will resort to really dangerous practices to find that acceptance.

Gerard was very young when I first met him and extremely naïve. He had recently discovered the dance scene and it was easy to tell that he was trying desperately to fit in. The group he was associating with was fairly hardcore and I very much doubted he would last for too long before lagging behind the others and dropping out.

Over the next couple of years I saw him a few times and he always seemed to be 'trying too hard'. I never asked him about his drug use but I was fairly sure that he was not keeping up with the others in his group. They were well known as a group who would try anything new and were now regularly experiencing a range of psychological and relationship problems. Anyone who tried to intervene was immediately regarded as an enemy and so I stood back.

When I discovered that Gerard had been arrested for dealing I was extremely surprised. I had no idea that he had been dealing and was angry at myself for not intervening sooner. His solicitor asked me to write a reference for Gerard, which I did, but it had little effect and the young man was jailed for four years.

Gerard wanted to be accepted by others. Even though they were definitely not worth it, he found what appeared to be a simple way of gaining his peer group's acceptance—supplying them with easy access to drugs.

Although the media (and many young people) would have you believe that 'drugs are everywhere', the truth is that for most people illicit drugs are pretty hard to come by.

I ask you the question: if you wanted to find a drug like cannabis, where would you go?

I'm imagining that you would most likely give the same response as the majority of Australians—you wouldn't have a clue! If you believe what you see on TV or in the movies you would just drive down the road to the local street drug market and pick up a 'stash' or pay a visit to the local dealer. But most people have no idea who their local dealer is, or if one even exists. The same applies to young people.

Many young people, like their parents, do not associate with illicit drug users, and as a result they would have no idea where to get drugs such as cannabis or ecstasy. However, they may know someone who knows someone who has a contact somewhere. Because of the illicit nature of drugs, contacts within friendship groups are the usual way that these substances are bought and sold. That is the way it has been for a long time and there is no sign that it is likely to change anytime in the future.

• What are recreational drugs?

Put simply, there is no such thing as a recreational drug. It is a term that I have never seen used in the scientific literature and no person who knows what they're talking about would ever use it. Politicians and the media use it frequently, then bluster that the term is inappropriate—when it is really only they who use it!

The term 'recreational' is used to describe drugs that are perceived to be less problematic than others—so-called 'party' drugs like ecstasy and amphetamines (or 'speed'). This is similar to using terminology such as 'soft drugs' and 'hard drugs' to categorise particular substances as less or more harmful, although it is not quite clear on what basis these assumptions are made. Once again, as far as I'm aware, these are not terms that are used by anyone who knows what they're talking about.

Although there is no such thing as a recreational drug, there *is* recreational drug use. Maybe that seems like semantics, but there really is a huge difference. So what is recreational drug use? And how does it differ from other forms of drug use? Essentially, although the drugs can change, there have been five patterns of use identified:

- *Experimental use*: This is usually motivated by curiosity and a desire to experience the effects the user has heard about. Experimental use generally occurs in social settings and among close friends and is limited in the number of times it occurs. An example could be a young girl having her first drink of alcohol at a party.
- *Recreational use* (also known as social–recreational use): This use tends to occur in social settings among friends who wish to share an experience. Unlike experimental use, which is limited to a few episodes, social use tends to be repeated regularly. A young man having a puff on a bong at a mate's place on a Saturday night is an example of recreational use.
- *Circumstantial–situational use*: This usually takes place in response to a specific situation. A great example of this is the person who can't have a drink without lighting up a cigarette. The smoking of the cigarette is defined as circumstantial use.
- *Intensive use*: This is long-term patterned drug use at least once a day. This type of use takes place to relieve a persistent problem or stressful situation or a desire to maintain a certain self-prescribed level of performance. A cocaine user who takes the drug to keep himself alert at work would be an example of this type of drug use.
- *Dependent or compulsive use*: Drug use that is completely out of control and even though the user is experiencing problems he or she continues to use. Compulsive users often keep using to prevent withdrawal. This is the most widely discussed type of drug use, with an example being a heroin user who needs to inject regularly.

Recreational drug use does not describe the drug, rather it examines the *way* a drug is used. A person who is demonstrating recreational drug use may eventually start to use it intensively or compulsively—it all depends on the person and the situation they find themselves in. Of course, there are some drugs that by their very nature (i.e. their addictive qualities) are more likely to lead to dependent use than others, such as heroin. Others are far more likely to be used in an experimental way due to their availability and effect, such as magic mushrooms and inhalants.

Where the confusion comes in is that a drug like ecstasy is much more likely to be used in a recreational (or social–recreational) manner than, say, an intensive or dependent way (although it can happen in rare cases). It is usually used in a social setting among a group of friends who wish to share an experience and use is repeated regularly over time. Another important aspect of this pattern of drug use is that it is rare to see use escalate to abuse.

That said, ecstasy or any other drug should not be classified as a recreational drug. To describe drugs as 'recreational' is just as ludicrous as calling them 'intensive drugs', 'experimental drugs' or 'dependent drugs'.

2
ALCOHOL AND PARTIES

Alcohol and parties is a big area to cover, but it is one that has garnered a lot of community attention in recent years. Alcohol is a huge part of Australian culture and it would be difficult to identify any social gathering that takes place in this country where alcohol does not play a significant role. Whether it be a christening, a wedding, a funeral, a birthday party or just getting together with a few friends for dinner, alcohol is there and often consumed to excess.

Is it any wonder, then, that our young people regard alcohol as integral to their gatherings and celebrations as well? They learn from those around them and from a very early age we start teaching our children that, as adults, we really are unable to celebrate without having a drink. Try to think of the last social get-together you attended where alcohol was not present. Unless the last event you went to was the local Alcoholics Anonymous (AA) meeting, I very much doubt whether you can come up with one.

A number of years ago a colleague and I were commissioned by a school to interview an entire school community about their alcohol use, as well as their attitudes towards the drug. A survey was designed and administered to every student from year five upwards, as well as all the teachers and the parent group. One of the most interesting results was in response to the question 'How important a role do you believe alcohol plays in a celebration?'

People responding to the survey could answer 'not at all important', 'not important', 'important', 'very important' or 'extremely important'.

As far as the younger students were concerned this was not an issue. They regarded alcohol as 'not important at all' when it came to having a good time. This didn't change until the last few years of high school, where it began to be regarded as 'important'. However, there were only two groups where a significant proportion believed that alcohol played a 'very important' or 'extremely important' role in celebrating—the parents and the teachers!

As I always say, our young people learn from somewhere and we are very good teachers, even when we don't want to be.

Sometimes things come out of left field that completely surprise me and challenge much of what I believe to be true. The following story is a great example of that . . .

A school prefect, Pat, came up and spoke to me after a school presentation to let me know about a night he would never forget. I had just finished giving a talk about the harms associated with alcohol and, as always, had shared many of the stories that I had come across in my travels.

Earlier in the year Pat had decided to party with two girls from his year group. They were all sixteen and fairly seasoned drinkers. Before they began their drinking session they each took a number of No-Doze tablets. Pat remembers taking three of the pills but said that the two girls he was with took a far greater number than that. The idea behind the caffeine tablets was to reduce the depressant effect of the alcohol. They would, they reasoned, be able to drink more and not feel as drunk.

They started to drink by playing a shots game with bourbon. After a couple of rounds each they were starting to feel quite merry and moved on to the next stage of their dangerous evening. A 750-ml bottle of whisky was brought out and Pat proceeded to skol the entire bottle. To ensure that this moment would be remembered for posterity, one of the girls recorded it on a mobile phone camera. Pat informed me, quite proudly, that it had now been posted on the YouTube website.

After the contents of the bottle had been downed the young man didn't feel so well. Eventually he stumbled to the bathroom. When he reached it his knees buckled under him and he fell to the floor, hitting his head on the tiles. His head split open and he started to vomit.

He remembers little else of the night, and the rest of the information about the evening was provided by one of the two girls present. They became worried about their friend, who was now lying on the bathroom floor, bleeding from the head. Instead of calling an ambulance, one of the girls decided to drive him to the local hospital herself. Obviously extremely intoxicated, but totally ignoring the risks, the girls put Pat into the car and made the trip.

Pat was kept in hospital overnight and, luckily, made a full recovery.

This was one of the strangest stories I have ever been told by a young person—not just because of the events he described, but because of how he now viewed the experience. He wanted me to use the story to warn others about the risks involved with drinking too much and made it quite clear that since the night in question he had drunk alcohol only a few times, and always in moderation. However, he was extremely proud of the fact that his skolling experience was posted on the internet and that it had been viewed by many. He could even tell me how many hits the video had received on the website. There was no shame, no stigma associated with the incident. When I asked him how he felt about spending a night in the emergency department, he brushed the question to one side. He saw the whole experience as a major achievement—one which, thanks to the mobile phone camera, others could relive in the future.

One of the most significant changes I have seen in the Australian community over the last decade or so has been the growing acceptance of public drunkenness. Getting drunk is often viewed as a 'badge of honour' and unfortunately Pat's story, although extreme, is not unique. The challenge that faces parents and educators in the coming years is to get the message across to young people and the community in general that drinking for intoxication is not acceptable and is potentially life-threatening. It's not going to be easy but it's worth a go!

This chapter looks at a range of questions dealing with alcohol and parties. In the last few years I have seen an incredible change in the type of questions I get asked in school communities, by both parents and their children. The most significant of these changes has been the number of alcohol-related questions compared to questions about other drug issues. In reality, alcohol has always been most important to the students I deal with, but it is now far more pronounced than ever before. Alcohol is the drug our kids and their friends are most likely to come into contact with during the teenage years and beyond, and without any doubt it is a drug they have problems with.

Many of the parents' questions relate to concerns raised in the media about teenage parties, binge drinking and events like Schoolies Week. None of these are particularly new phenomena, but due to the increased media attention and the way some of the stories are presented, it appears to many parents that this pattern of teenage drinking is completely new and 'out of control'. As far as I'm aware there is no evidence to support the claims that we have more young people drinking alcohol than ever before. There is definitely a group of adolescents who are drinking in very dangerous ways and they appear to be indulging in more risky practices as time goes on, but is this group growing in size? Once again, I know of no evidence to suggest that this is the case. Most of our young people are trying to do the right thing.

The young people's questions continue to relate to issues around personal safety. Something that many parents forget is that for most adolescents the only drug emergency that they will ever experience will be to do with alcohol. Like their parents before them, they will either have to look after a drunk friend who is vomiting, call an ambulance for someone who has lost consciousness, or simply sit with a best friend who bit off a little more than they could chew and found themselves feeling rather unwell.

Looking after someone who is drunk is traumatic enough for an adult. For an adolescent with not much life experience and little information this can be a major life event. We need to be sure that we arm our young people with as much information and practical advice as we possibly can, regardless of whether they are drinkers or not. They need good-quality information about what to do in an emergency.

Teenage parties can be dangerous places. There is often inadequate adult supervision, young people tend to drink more than they would in other environments and those people who are around them are often ill-equipped to deal with an emergency. The information provided in this chapter is intended to help you to understand what you should be doing as a parent to support your child, and also give you an insight into the type of information your child really needs to help them survive the teenage party scene.

• How should I introduce alcohol to my child?

Alcohol is a big part of many of our lives. We drink to celebrate a victory, we drink to commiserate a loss, we drink when a baby is born, we drink when someone dies. It should come as no surprise that when our young people approach adulthood they start to experiment with alcohol. They have watched their parents and other adults socialise for many years and on a great number of occasions alcohol has been an integral part of the event.

The issue of alcohol and young people is one that attracts a great deal of attention and concern. It is also an extremely complicated area and one that we are learning more about all the time. Many parents are looking for guidance on how to deal with alcohol in their family, particularly as we continue to see people start their drinking career at an increasingly younger age. Some of the questions that I am asked by parents include:

- How and when should I introduce alcohol to my child?
- Are there things that I can do to prevent my child drinking in the future?
- What behaviours of mine are more likely to cause my child to drink heavily in the future?

Unfortunately, many parents believe that there is little they can do to influence their child's drinking behaviour. Some believe that drinking and getting drunk occasionally is just a phase that all teenagers go through and that it is merely a rite of passage into adulthood. This is not true. We know that there are some young people who don't go through that phase, and sending a message out there that all of them do is dangerous. Research has shown us that parents can make a real difference when it comes to alcohol consumption, particularly if they really put their mind to it.

One of the most worrying things that I have noticed over the years is that parents now want to be their child's best friend rather than their parent. Each time I hear a parent say, 'We're just not friends at the moment . . .' I want to clip them across the ear and yell: 'You're not meant to be their friend, you're their parent!' Your child has the opportunity to make lots of friends in their lives—they only get one set of parents and you are it! The fear that you may damage your relationship with your child if you act like a parent, particularly if you dare to say no to them, is irrational. Young people need parents to give them guidance and to set rules and boundaries around a wide range of activities, including alcohol use. Although teenagers may not always like the rules that are set, they are necessary and assist them to socialise with others in a responsible and healthy way.

Just think about it from a workplace perspective. Where is a better place to work—at a job where the boss doesn't show any interest in what you do and lets you do whatever you want, or one where you have been set clear boundaries and you know what you are expected to do in order to succeed? A child needs to feel the same way. Having a parent who is constantly saying 'yes' may feel great for a while, but in the end the child learns little about boundaries and can end up finding it extremely difficult to function productively in the real world.

There are a number of simple parenting tips that, if followed, will enable you to have a positive influence on your children's future alcohol use. The first thing to note is that parents who are aware of what activities their teenagers take part in and take an active interest in what they do, who talk and listen to their children and model positive behaviour towards alcohol, are likely to have a far more positive effect on their children's future drinking. Of course, parents don't operate in a vacuum; there are many other social influences that come into play. However, parents should never underestimate the very real influence they can have in this area.

So let's look a little more closely at some of the things that parents can do that will influence their child's alcohol consumption.

Monitor your children

If you ask the parent of a primary school-aged child where their child is at any point in time they would nearly always know exactly where they are. They monitor them closely, making sure they know their movements as well as who their friends are. This begins to change in the early years of high school. Many parents say they just get tired and their child is older and needs to be treated more like an adult. However, it is worth the effort to monitor your teenager well. Young people raised by parents who are well aware of what their children are up to and who they are with have been shown to start drinking at a later age, tend to drink less, and are less likely to develop problematic drinking patterns in the future.

Parental relationships

It is vital that you try to maintain a positive and open relationship with your child through this time. It's not always going to be easy but the ability to communicate any concerns you may have about the activities they are involved in is essential. Children who feel they are able to talk candidly with their parents about a range of issues are more likely to drink in moderation or not drink at all compared to young people who do not have such good relationships with their parents.

Parental behaviour management

Most parents use one or more of a variety of strategies to manage their child's behaviour. These strategies can include the use of incentives, positive reinforcement and simply making sure their child knows that there are consequences for misbehaviour. It doesn't take a genius to work out which strategies are more likely to result in positive outcomes. Once again, I come back to the workplace scenario to illustrate this important point. Which workplace is more likely to result in happier employees and increased productivity: is it going to be one with no rules and no direction, or the workplace where the people in charge sit down with the employees and come to an agreement on appropriate rules and behaviours, or a dictatorship where strict rules are imposed without discussion?

Research has shown that parents who set positive family standards and rules, reward good behaviour and use negotiation skills appear to be able to delay the age their child starts to drink. Strict discipline and lots of conflict in the home is linked to higher rates of teenage alcohol use. At the other extreme, the children of parents who appear to be more tolerant of teenage drinking tend to drink more.

Parents' drinking behaviour

From a very early age young people are bombarded with messages, both positive and negative, from the people around them regarding acceptable behaviour. Young people's drinking behaviour is no exception and often emulates that of their parents. That is, if adults drink more, so do their children. Positive role-modelling is possibly the most important tool a parent has to convey information to their child about alcohol and its use.

Parents' involvement in the introduction of alcohol
to their children

And now we come down to trying to answer the original question. How parents choose to introduce their child to alcohol does appear to affect the attitude the young person has towards alcohol and their future drinking patterns, but the relationship is complex and we still have a long way to go before we have any clear answers.

We are still finding out the best way for parents to introduce alcohol to their children. At present, the results of research are often contradictory. On the one hand, there is research to suggest that parents can have a positive influence on their child's drinking behaviour by allowing them small amounts of alcohol and trusting their child's ability to act responsibly and drink in moderation. That said, it is important to bear in mind that if parents do not set boundaries around drinking, their child is likely to drink more. On the other hand, other studies suggest that introducing your child to alcohol at an early age, even in a family context, could lead to future binge drinking.

One thing, however, is now becoming extremely clear. We now know more than ever before about the effect of alcohol on the developing brain, and all experts agree that teenagers under sixteen years of age should avoid alcohol.

We also know that it is important to delay the initiation of alcohol for as long as you can for several other reasons. The earlier a child starts using alcohol, for example, the greater the possibility that they will develop problems with the drug in the future. The message to parents about the introduction of alcohol is clear: hold off for as long as you can!

This is a relatively new message. For years, when I was asked how and when to introduce alcohol to children, I would respond by saying, 'Before someone else does and as early as you think appropriate—perhaps at a family meal.' Due to the new information we now have that message has changed dramatically. You still want to try to ensure that your child's first drink isn't consumed at a park late on a Saturday night, but providing that drink too early, without setting clear rules and boundaries at the same time, is likely to be just as problematic in other ways.

The most important factor to remember here is 'individual difference'. When I say that I am not talking about the adolescent, I am talking about the family. Alcohol plays a different role in every family and that needs to be considered when planning how to introduce alcohol to your child.

Here are stories from three Australian families that illustrate my point:

> During a parent information evening I began to talk about my views on the introduction of alcohol in the family home. Halfway through I was interrupted by a woman in the back row. She said that my advice was impractical and would not work in her family.
>
> She was a mother of three and had introduced alcohol to her children at a very young age—all pre-teen. She and her husband were not big drinkers but enjoyed a glass of wine or two with their meal every night and provided positive role models to their children. They were of Italian descent and this is how they had been introduced to alcohol when they were younger; neither she nor, to the best of her knowledge, any of her siblings had ever indulged in binge drinking.
>
> All I could do was reiterate that every family is different, with different views and experiences, and every parent was going to have their own opinion on how to handle this complex issue. I was told later that the woman owned a vineyard!

In a family such as this it would be almost impossible to delay the onset of alcohol use until the kids' late teens. They have most probably been brought up with activities such as wine tasting and would likely regard alcohol in a very different way to the vast majority of young people of their age.

We hear many people from a Mediterranean background discuss how alcohol was introduced in their family as they were growing up. In countries such as Italy and Greece, alcohol is introduced to children at a very young age with a meal. It is done in a very matter-of-fact way and there is evidence to support that this led to more responsible alcohol use later in life. The problem is that the 'Mediterranean model' is very difficult to transplant into the Australian experience. There are so many other cultural influences that come into play in this country (alcohol's link with sport and celebrating, for example) that expecting what worked for you and your family in the past will work in a different time and place is, frankly, wishful thinking.

Maureen was the mother of a fifteen-year-old boy. She and her husband contacted me after hearing me speak at their son's school. Now that their son was getting to an age where he would be exposed to alcohol they wanted advice on how to deal with the issue.

Neither Maureen nor her husband had ever drunk alcohol. It had never been part of their lives. Neither of them was particularly religious, and they didn't view alcohol in a negative light—they just didn't drink!

Should they start having a glass of wine with a meal? They had heard that one of the best ways to introduce alcohol to a child was at the family dinner table—was that the most appropriate thing for them to do?

This story almost broke my heart. Maureen and her husband felt totally isolated and were desperately trying to figure out how to approach an issue they had no practical experience with. This is a great example of individual difference. Alcohol was not a part of this family's experience and their son had most probably learned an enormous amount from his parents about the importance (or lack of importance) of alcohol from observing how they socialised over the years.

Should they bring alcohol into the home to introduce their son to drink? Absolutely not! They have taught their child a great deal in their decision not to drink and it is highly likely that this will affect how he chooses to consume alcohol in the future. It doesn't necessarily mean he is never going to drink, it's just that he will have a different perception of the importance of alcohol in day-to-day family life.

Once again, there is no escaping the other cultural influences that are all around. There will be social pressures on Maureen's son to drink and he will probably learn the hard way about limits, but the modelling of behaviour and attitudes he has observed through the years will no doubt provide a very strong foundation for his future.

I was called to a school where they had been having problems with teenage parties. It had been brought to the principal's attention that at several sixteen-year-olds' birthday parties the parents had decided to serve alcohol to those attending and, in two cases, a keg of beer was provided. A parent forum was planned and the principal had insisted that some of the parents concerned attend.

It was not a comfortable evening and tempers were definitely running high. The vast majority of parents at the forum believed that providing alcohol to sixteen-year-olds was unacceptable, however there were others who saw it very differently. The father who had provided the keg for his son's sixteenth birthday party was angry that he had been forced to come to the forum and insisted that he had every right to do what he had done.

He told the audience that he had been introduced to alcohol by his father in his early teens and that it had done him no harm. He wanted to make sure that his son had a great birthday and in his view the sixteenth birthday was as significant as the twenty-first was to the previous generation. He explained that he had done everything he could to make the evening as safe as possible. The young people were monitored, security was employed to deal with gatecrashers and, in his opinion, the night went off without a hitch.

There were so many times in the evening that I wanted to say, 'So it did you no harm? This coming from someone who is providing a keg to a group of sixteen-year-olds!'

This was not a father who 'didn't care'. He did what he thought was right given the information and experience he had. Maybe he was right; maybe the way he was introduced to alcohol by his father didn't do him any harm—I have no idea about his personal alcohol use. Regardless of that, what worked for you may not necessarily work for your child. We also know so much more now than we did even ten years ago, and providing alcohol to adolescents in this way is not the way to go.

I am sure this father had the best intentions. According to him, he had tried to keep the party as safe as possible. But what was the most powerful message he sent his son about alcohol that night? It was: 'to celebrate you need alcohol'. Is that really the message you want to send your child when you introduce them to the drug that we know contributes to more young people dying than any other?

Examine the place that alcohol holds in your home and how its use is being modelled. Then negotiate rules and boundaries with your teenager. Obviously, young people need to learn to drink responsibly. Is a teenage party the best place for this to occur? Most probably not. I'd say one of the best ways to teach children about responsible alcohol use is for parents to set the example of how, where and why to consume alcohol.

• What should I do if my child wants to attend parties where alcohol may be served?

One of the most challenging times for parents is when their child is invited to their first teenage party. As scary as they may seem to parents, parties are extremely important for young people. They provide them with valuable opportunities to develop the skills they need in order to socialise and relate effectively with their peers. Unfortunately, in recent years fewer and fewer parents are prepared to host teenage parties due to fears that they will end up spiralling out of control. The media has let us know about so many parties that began innocently enough but ended up with hundreds of drunken teenagers, most of them uninvited, spilling out onto the streets wreaking havoc. As a result, it really is a very brave parent who makes the decision to hold a party in their home.

That said, it is important for parents to remember that plenty of uneventful teenage parties are held every weekend right across the country.

> Sally's daughter Sophie was about to turn sixteen and she wanted a party. When it came to running such an event Sally was totally lacking experience. She had difficulty remembering the parties she attended during her adolescence but was worried due to all of the media stories about teenage drinking and police involvement.
>
> Sally did everything right. She planned the party together with her daughter, got the best advice from a number of people and did her very best to ensure that the night would run as smoothly as possible. Alcohol was not served and that was made extremely clear to all those invited.
>
> To her surprise the night went without a hitch! There were no drunken teenagers, no vomiting, no destruction of property and the police didn't need to be called. Sophie and the friends she invited had a great time, and Sally's faith in young people was restored.

Of course there are some parents who are not as lucky as Sally. Sometimes things go wrong no matter what precautions you take, but in my experience those parents who plan carefully and involve their child in the entire process usually have an experience that is not overly traumatic!

As frightening as it is for the parents hosting a party, many parents would agree that it is equally worrying to have a child invited to one. Whether to allow your child to attend a party or not is a decision that all parents will face eventually—and you'll be making your decision on the basis of information that can be extremely difficult to collect.

One thing I can guarantee is that your child will not want you to contact the parents holding the party. As far as a teenager is concerned that is the ultimate embarrassment. However, if you want to make an informed decision when it comes to your child attending a party or not, you are going to have to bite the bullet.

If your child was going on a school excursion and there were any potential risks involved you would want to know as much as possible about the activity they were taking part in. The school would provide information on where the students were going and let you know what precautions they were taking to make the trip as safe as they could. If you felt that the trip was too risky, you would refuse permission for your child to take part. That is your right as a parent. It should be exactly the same for a teenage party.

Make sure you know what type of event your child is going to attend. Ask your child questions about the party and where it is being held. Get as much information as you can, and don't just rely on what your child is willing and able to tell you. Even though you may have the most trusting relationship with your child, I would suggest that you are not going to get the whole story from them—not that they would necessarily lie to you, but chances are they really don't know themselves. As a parent you need to go to the source: the other parents.

It never ceases to amaze me how many parents do not find out more about where their teenager is going on a Saturday night. Of course, contacting a parent you don't know and asking them questions about a party they are holding is not necessarily going to be an easy task, but that's what parenting is all about—a whole pile of not very easy tasks! However, you may be surprised at the reception you get and in fact it could be quite rewarding.

I had given a presentation at a well-known girls school in Sydney a number of months before and had been invited back to speak at a mothers' breakfast meeting. When the talk finished a mother came up to introduce herself. Ruth was the mother of a sixteen-year-old girl, Marta. She told me that when I had last spoken at the school, one message in particular had resonated with her—develop a parents network. If your child gets invited to a party, contact the parents hosting the event and find out what is going on.

'Now, whenever my daughter gets invited to a party, I always call the parents,' Ruth told me. 'I haven't been exactly popular with Marta but it's been a tremendous experience for me.

'Without exception I have been greeted by parents only too pleased to take my call and let me know what they have planned. In fact, many of the parents are relieved to hear from me, sometimes saying that they were getting worried that no one seemed to care.'

Unfortunately, not everyone will have the same experience as Ruth. As I said, contacting parents you do not know and asking them questions about how they are going to host a teenage party can be very difficult, and you might find yourself treading on toes.

Lorraine has two children. She works in the field of health promotion in a regional area so has a good knowledge of the potential harm of teenage drinking. She frequently gives advice to parents about having greater involvement in their children's lives and monitoring them more effectively. When it came to her own teenage son she thought she had better practise what she preached.

Lorraine's son was invited to a party and she decided to contact the parents who were hosting the event. She realised that she needed to be careful how she broached the subject, and before she made the call she planned what she would say very carefully.

The call began very positively. Lorraine had decided to ease into the questioning by saying that she had made the call to get directions on how to find the property. This was received very well. The next question—Lorraine asked whether the parents were going to be supervising the party—was answered politely by the other mother. However things took a turn for the worse when Lorraine asked whether there was going to be alcohol supplied.

The woman on the other end of the phone turned on Lorraine. 'Who the hell are you to ask me that?' the mother yelled. 'What's the matter, lady? Don't you trust your son enough to let him go to a party?'

The abuse went on for some time. Obviously Lorraine had touched on a sensitive issue. She tried to calm the woman down, but to no avail; she continued to yell, attempting to twist Lorraine's genuine concern for her son's safety into a lack of parental trust. Lorraine put the phone down and let her son know that he would definitely not be attending the party.

When you contact a parent to ask them about their party make sure you plan what you are going to say beforehand. Write down the questions you are going to ask and make sure your tone is not confrontational or accusatory.

Some of the questions that you want answered might include the following:

- Will there be adult supervision? Does this mean actual supervision or will there just be adults in the house?
- Who are the adults?
- Will you be providing alcohol?
- What will you be doing about underage drinking?

There are plenty of other questions that you could ask and if you have an existing relationship with the hosts I would strongly advise that you ask them, if only to ensure that they have thought all possible scenarios through. However, if you do not know the parents they could take offence at a complete stranger asking them such questions as:

- How do you plan to deal with uninvited guests?
- Have you registered your party with the local police?
- Have you got plans in case things get out of control?

Some of the ways you could approach the subject when you make the call could include the following:

- 'My son has just started going to parties and I'm still trying to negotiate my way through setting some ground rules. I'm just calling to find out how you're dealing with the alcohol issue.'
- 'Thank you so much for inviting my daughter to the party. We have some basic rules around parties and alcohol that we have developed and we just want some information about what will be happening on the night.'
- 'I know it can be very difficult to host a party and I really do appreciate that you are offering your home to the young people. We're considering holding an event in the future, and I'm interested to know what you're doing about adult supervision and alcohol use?'

It is important to remember that every family is different and that not every parent is going to have the same views as you on the issue of teenagers and alcohol. If they do have a different viewpoint, this phone call is definitely not the time for you to give them a lecture on what you believe is the right way to bring up a child. Thank them for their time, wish them luck for the evening and get off the phone. Getting into a dispute about the right way to hold a teenage party is not necessary. Like Lorraine in the story above, just thank your lucky stars that you did the right thing and have now prevented your child from getting into what you perceive to be a high-risk situation.

As a parent you can only do what you think is right for your child. How other parents raise their children is their business and it really is not your place to become involved in their parenting decisions. This will only change if during the course of your discussion you discover that there are young people at risk of experiencing harm, e.g. physical violence.

It isn't just what you do before the event that matters. You also need to be prepared for things that could occur during the evening that may also put your child at risk.

Catherine's daughter Lauren was fifteen years old and had been given permission to go to a party with some of her friends. One of the other mothers had agreed to take them there and it was Catherine's responsibility to pick them up. They had negotiated a time—eleven thirty—and Lauren left home just after eight. Catherine was extremely surprised to receive a call from her daughter at nine thirty, asking if she could pick the girls up early.

When Catherine asked what was wrong, Lauren told her that the mother of the teenager hosting the party had invited some of her male friends, all in their early thirties. Before long these guys became a little intoxicated and began to hit on the young women. Lauren and her friends had begun to feel uncomfortable and wanted out—and a quick call to her mother ensured a speedy retreat from an unpleasant experience.

Lauren responded in a very mature way to this very difficult situation. Even if you have called the parents before the party and gathered information about adult supervision, do you really know what the standard of supervision will be? Are the adults responsible and can you really entrust your child to people you do not know, particularly when alcohol is present?

Janine's son Luke was looking forward to one of his first teenage parties. His mother had been very thorough with her explanations about why she was worried about him attending and she had clearly explained the rules she and her husband had come up with around the subject. She would be contacting the parents of the child hosting the party, and if there was alcohol present he would not be allowed to go. If he was to go, one or both of his parents would be dropping him off and picking him up. Luke begrudgingly accepted the 'terms and conditions' and the plans were made for the big night.

Janine placed a call to the host parents and asked all of her planned questions. She was happy with the responses. This was a party celebrating a sixteenth birthday party and the parents would not be allowing alcohol in their home. There would be adult supervision and the party would finish at midnight.

On the night Janine arranged to take Luke and three of his friends to the party. It was 8.30 pm and there were already a number of teenagers outside the house. She had compromised and agreed not to take Luke to the door and meet the parents but reiterated to her son that she would be returning to pick him up at 11.30 pm.

At about 10.30 pm Janine received a call from her son. He told her that she would not need to pick him up from the party anymore and asked that when the time came could she pick him and his friends up from another address. Janine's response was swift and precise. 'Why did you leave the party when we had explicitly made arrangements for the evening?' she wanted to know.

Luke's response amazed her.

Apparently, the party had begun to get out of hand not long after her son had arrived. Gatecrashers, underage drinking and other inappropriate behaviour had led the parents hosting the party to shut it down before it got completely out of control. The music had been turned off and all the teenagers present had been asked to leave. The young people had been left to spill out onto the street and wander away. Luke and his friends made their way to the local golf course and decided to party there.

Janine immediately got into her car to fetch her son. She could not believe that he had been placed in such a dangerous situation by the parents hosting the party.

There is no way that you can be prepared for all of the possible scenarios that may occur when your child attends a teenage party.

However, it is vital that you realise that things can go wrong and do your best to outline some possible strategies that could keep your teenager safe in potentially dangerous situations. It is extremely important to discuss these with your child and let them know that, no matter what happens, they can contact you and you will be there for them.

Miriam had a fifteen-year-old daughter, Sarah, who had recently been invited to her first major party, which was being held a few suburbs away. Miriam agreed that her daughter could attend as long as a few basic rules were followed. One of these was that Miriam would drop her at the event and pick her up at the end of the evening, with the end of the evening being midnight. There was to be no alcohol consumed, as Sarah was underage, and, most importantly, if something went wrong, Sarah had to promise to contact her mother immediately.

Sarah agreed to the conditions and in the week leading up to the party Miriam went over and over the rules, particularly the last one. She did not want to get a call from a police station or an emergency department. Sarah's mother was to be the first port of call. No matter what her daughter got herself into, she wanted her daughter to trust her enough to call her if something went wrong.

On the night of the party, Miriam drove Sarah and a couple of her friends across town, all the way reminding her of her promise to call if she needed to. By this time Sarah appeared well and truly over it. There was no way that she would ever call her mum—that would be social suicide! When they arrived at the party, all seemed calm and the girls got out of the car, excited about the night ahead.

Miriam drove home, stopping briefly at a friend's house for a debriefing session, and was just pulling into her driveway when her phone rang. It was Sarah. She was crying and quite distressed. Apparently the party had got out of control not long after the girls arrived. A number of cars filled with gatecrashers had pulled up and the atmosphere changed dramatically. The police had been called and Sarah and her friends had realised that this was not the place for them.

Miriam rushed over to the party as fast as she could. Her daughter, now with a much larger group of friends, had arranged to meet her a few doors down from the party. By the time she arrived they were all anxious for a lift to a safer place. What made Miriam feel so fantastic was that she was the parent the girls had decided to call. Her message had got through and she was thrilled at the result.

What this story illustrates quite clearly is the importance of having a strong, positive relationship with your child, one in which they feel they are able to contact you without fear of getting into trouble.

There is a wonderful activity that you can use when setting some rules around parties. I developed it a number of years ago and have used it with many parents and have seen many successful outcomes.

When your child asks to go to a party tell them that you want to negotiate some rules and boundaries and make sure that they understand that you want to work with them on developing these. Find a quiet time, get a large sheet of paper and a pen and sit down with your child. Make sure you are not going to be disturbed. Draw a line down the middle of the piece of paper and ask them to write on one side of the line their 'wish list' when it comes to going to a party. I can't begin to imagine everything your child might say, but I can pretty well guarantee the list will include some of the following:

- *I don't want you to call the parents of the person having the party.*
- *I don't want you to drop me off.*
- *I don't want you to pick me up.*

- *I don't want you anywhere near the party.*
- *I want to be able to drink alcohol.*
- *I want to come home on Thursday!*

Give them lots of time and make sure they include everything they want, no matter how minute the detail. Once they have finished, take the pen and tell them that you are now going to write down all of the things that you want. Having done this for some time with parents I rarely see parents write anything more than one word—*safety*.

Now hand the pen back to your child and explain to them that both sides will have to compromise so that each can have as many of the things written on their wish list as possible. I have yet to see this process backfire. In fact, it is quite amazing to see the teenager take the pen and start crossing items off his or her list. Inevitably, you are left with a couple of statements on the child's side and that is where negotiation comes into play. Now that the child has an understanding of where you are coming from this process is usually much easier and the development of some rules and boundaries that both parties are satisfied with is far less stressful.

Be a parent when it comes to parties, particularly for the first couple of years. Take an interest in where your kids are going and who they will be with, and do a little bit of parenting when it comes to finding out what type of party it will be and whether there will be alcohol present. Make your decision on whether or not they should attend based on good information and involve your child in that decision. Let them know why you made the decision that you did.

Most importantly, when they are at the party continue to be a parent. Make sure you are available to them should they need you. Your child should feel comfortable calling you in any situation, at any time. As a woman I know says to her children at every opportunity, 'You can call me anytime, anywhere and I will be there to pick you up, no questions asked . . . then!'

• How can I make sure that a party I hold for my teenager doesn't get out of control?

Holding a party for teenagers, whether it be at your home or somewhere you have hired for the evening, is a huge responsibility. We know young people begin to drink much earlier than they used to and that makes the decision to host a party much more difficult. However, it is important to remember that holding a party can also be a great opportunity for you to strengthen your relationship with your child, get to know their friends and become more involved in their life. However, given all of the negative media attention in this area it is no surprise that many parents opt not to hold parties, fearing that they will inevitably lead to alcohol-fuelled mayhem.

Over the years I have worked with many promoters to help them run dance events at nightclubs or festivals. Although these people often get a lot of bad publicity, in my experience most of them try extremely hard to provide a safe environment for their clientele. They have no choice; they operate under a microscope, with the media keen to pounce on them if they don't do the right thing. Besides, they would not be allowed to run an event unless they followed some basic rules. This usually involves liquor licensing regulations, a whole range of safety rules involving fire and law-enforcement requirements, security and medical provision. Many of them do much more than the minimum required because they want to do the right thing and look after the people attending their events.

Parents holding a party for teenagers need to think in a similar way. You are providing an environment for a group of young people to get together and have a good time. Things can go wrong. You need to think about all the possible risks and make sure that the party is as safe as possible—for the people coming to the party, your neighbours and, of course, you and your family. But there are no guarantees. No matter what safeguards you put in place there is always the possibility that something could go wrong. However, the greater the planning, the more likely it is that things will run smoothly.

It is also extremely important to involve your child in the planning of the party. You can bet that they will have a long list of requirements for what makes a successful evening and together you will need to make many decisions about a wide range of issues, including the provision of alcohol. As much as it is important to have your child's input so that the party can be successful, it is also helpful for your child to be aware of all the planning and hard work that needs to be done to ensure that the night turns out well. They are then much more likely to appreciate the efforts that have been made by all involved and work cooperatively to resolve challenging issues.

Joel had asked his parents, Rosemary and Bob, if he could have a party at home for his sixteenth birthday. Both of them were quite worried about the potential risks. They had friends who had held a party for their daughter the previous year and had a great deal of trouble. Underage drinkers, gatecrashers and associated violence had led to the local police being called and the party subsequently closed down. Rosemary and Bob definitely didn't want a repeat performance but they firmly believed that young people needed to have parties. Their greatest concern was that if they didn't provide a safe environment for their son and his friends, they would go and party in a public place instead. They agreed to host a party as long as Joel assisted them in the organisation.

They gathered literature on holding a teenage party from a range of agencies, including the Department of Education and the Police Service. They sat with Joel and together they listed all of the things that could go wrong. As you can imagine the list was fairly long and pretty scary. In fact, it was so scary that Joel decided he didn't want a party after all! He had seen the risks involved and made the decision that having a party was not worth it.

Rosemary and Bob insisted that it was not their intention to try to get Joel to change his mind about a party. In fact, they tried to convince him to reconsider! But Joel was adamant, and in the end he celebrated his birthday by going camping with a few mates instead.

I'm not suggesting that you involve your child in the organisation of a party in order to frighten them into dropping the idea, but this example does show that young people are often unaware of the huge responsibility that goes with hosting such an event. They do need to know that there is a great deal of work that goes into a successful and safe party. As much as your child will benefit from the socialising aspect of attending a party with their friends, they will also learn a great deal by helping to put an event together.

Some of the decisions that should be made with your child include the following.

What food will be available?

Parties need food, particularly if alcohol is going to be served, as it slows down the amount of alcohol people drink. But you need to avoid having too much salty food which could make people thirsty and thus likely to drink more. Your child will know what food is 'socially acceptable' to the current generation of young people and will be of great assistance here.

Will alcohol be allowed and who will serve it if it is?

This question is definitely going to be the tough one for most families. If you do make the decision to serve alcohol, how are you going to deal with your underage guests, remembering the legal restrictions that exist in some parts of the country on providing alcohol to minors? If a parent contacts you to ask you about alcohol are you prepared to defend your decision? Does your child understand the risks involved? Are guests going to be able to bring their own and drink as much as they want or will there be someone serving alcohol, monitoring how much people are drinking?

If you decide on an alcohol-free party, how will you handle guests who turn up with alcohol?

Once again, this will be a difficult one for parents and teenage children to negotiate. Your child will not want to be embarrassed by having their parents confiscate alcohol from friends who arrive with a bottle. If you decide to make the party alcohol-free then a solution to this sort of problem needs to be worked out carefully beforehand. Simply turning a guest away from the party is not a good option. You do not know whether the young person has been dropped off at your home by their parent and how they're getting home—maybe the parents are returning in a few hours. Sending kids off into the night with a bottle of something is irresponsible and dangerous. Discuss this with your teenager and see if you can come up with some ideas for dealing with this problem together.

How will you handle gatecrashers?

Gatecrashers are now a fact of life at teenage parties, particularly if you are providing alcohol. In the age of mobile phones and SMS messaging it doesn't take long for the word to get out that there is a party happening. Will you be handing out invitations to those people who you want to come or will you have a guest list? Will you be hiring security to manage the party or do you have a couple of burly relatives who can handle a sticky situation? What responsibility will your teenager have in looking after the door, particularly considering that they are more likely to know who was invited and who wasn't?

What will you do in an emergency?

The best-planned parties can still end up with an emergency of some description. This does not have to be related to alcohol—when a group of people get together, no matter what their age, things can go wrong. Who will take responsibility should something go wrong? Who will compile the list of emergency numbers and where will it be kept? Discuss with your teenager the necessity of registering your party with the local police and why it is so important. When you do register your party, make sure you do it together so that they can see and understand the process.

How will the guests be getting home and what time will the party be finishing?

Unbelievably, this is one aspect of a hosting a teenage party that many parents forget about. It is undoubtedly one of the most difficult to police but it needs to be discussed with your child so that they understand the huge responsibility you have taken on. There is no way that you are able to know how each and every guest attending the party is getting home, but if something happens to any of those young people when they leave your house, particularly if they have been drinking, it would be hard to live with yourself. Stress the importance of having a strict finishing time for the party and advertise that time widely. This will ensure that the guests' parents are aware that their children will be asked to leave your home at a particular time. Hopefully this will reduce the number of teenagers spilling out onto the street and into the parks and other public spaces in your local area after the party has finished.

But as the saying goes, the best-laid plans of mice and men . . . Sometimes things go wrong even when you have done everything right.

When it came to celebrating her son's sixteenth birthday, Leonie agreed to hold a party. Her decision was made easier when her neighbour suggested that they hold a joint event, as her son was also celebrating a birthday.

Leonie lived on a large property and her home was spacious enough to host a great party but she knew that she had to do a good deal of organising to make it as safe as possible. There was a lot of discussion about issues such as adult supervision and whether alcohol would be supplied, and it was finally decided that adults (many of the parents of the teenagers attending) would be invited and there would be no underage drinking permitted.

On the evening of the party some of the young people arrived with their parents and it was decided that the adults would stay on one side of the house so the teenagers could have some privacy. However, all partygoers were checked for alcohol before they were allowed in and Leonie and other parents regularly moved through the area, usually on the pretext of supplying more food to the teens.

Things seemed to be going well until Leonie noticed that she couldn't see several of her son's friends. She asked some of the others where they were and she was told that they had taken a walk away from the house. She then began to monitor the party a little more closely.

Soon she noticed that young people would take it in turns to go out into the garden in pairs. One of these pairings was of particular concern to Leonie—two fourteen-year-old girls took a trip down to the back of the property and when Leonie followed them she found them taking hefty swigs from a bottle of tequila. She immediately took the bottle and tipped the contents down the sink, but unfortunately it was too late for one of the girls. She was already extremely drunk and getting worse. Leonie had to call the girl's mother.

Around this time she also noticed that there were a number of young people at the party who hadn't been invited. Together with some of the other adults present she approached these intruders and asked who had invited them.

'What's it to you, lady?' they responded.

Even though she had arranged to have a number of adults present and had banned alcohol, the night was not going as planned. It didn't become total chaos but a number of uninvited guests that were difficult to remove, as well as a number of very young drunken teenagers, made it a night that Leonie would rather forget.

Over the years I have met many parents eager to tell me their success stories when it comes to holding teenage parties. Most of these have involved the decision not to serve alcohol to underage teenagers. Once that decision has been made and the young person whose party it is has understood and accepted it, the night usually proceeds without incident. In reality, if alcohol is not permitted and everyone is made well aware of that and it is policed appropriately, gatecrashers are unlikely to turn up and those young people who are only interested in getting drunk will go somewhere else.

I can definitely understand some of the arguments that parents use when they agree to provide alcohol at teenage parties, particularly if they are hosting events for young adults who are close to the legal drinking age. However, many of the arguments put forward simply don't hold up under scrutiny. Possibly one of the most ridiculous is when parents say that they are providing a 'safe environment' in which their teenager can drink and that if they didn't their child would simply go off and drink somewhere else unsupervised.

I challenge any parent hosting a party where alcohol is being supplied to underage teenagers to prove that they are providing a 'safe environment'. Even in licensed premises where alcohol is kept behind a bar and strict rules around responsible service govern how it is provided to patrons, it can be extremely difficult for staff to keep track of how much people have been drinking. How, then, can a parent hosting a party really supervise a number of teenagers and ensure that they are drinking responsibly?

You are sending a very strong message to your child when you agree to provide alcohol to minors. Most importantly, you are telling them to ignore the law—alcohol is an illegal drug for those under the age of eighteen. The laws are different across the country, with New South Wales having the strictest laws in this area, but what you are saying to your child when you provide alcohol at an underage party is that although you want them to obey other laws, this one they can ignore!

If you allow your child to drink alcohol in your home with a family meal or even at a family get-together, that is your choice as a parent. But providing alcohol to young people at a party is very different. There are very few parents who want their children to drink alcohol to excess. Almost every parent who gives their teenager alcohol to take to a party or provides it to those attending a party they are hosting does it for the right reasons. Often parents will say to me that they make it very clear to their child that they don't want them to drink alcohol as they're handing over the bottles or giving them the money to buy it, somehow thinking that this is going to have some sort of positive outcome. In fact the only message the child picks up is 'my parents gave me alcohol'. This tacit approval plays an important role in how your child views alcohol.

There is no handbook on how to be the perfect parent, nor is there one on holding an incident-free teenage party. There are definitely some guidelines that you can follow, some of which have been outlined above. Without doubt, the best thing you can do to reduce risk is to make the event alcohol-free. If you believe that this is not an option for your child at their stage of development, make sure you take every precaution to make the party as safe as possible for all concerned.

• Why can't girls drink as much as boys?

This may seem like some sort of male conspiracy but the truth is that alcohol affects women more than men. Research continues to reveal more and more health risks for women who drink compared to men, and that is why we are so concerned about the increasing number of young women who drink to excess.

Due to their smaller size, body type and the way they absorb and metabolise alcohol, on average women are affected by alcohol more quickly than men and are more vulnerable to the harmful effects. Studies have found that women who drink face a greater risk of developing diseases related to alcohol abuse, such as liver disease, heart disease and cancer (particularly breast cancer), than men who drink similar amounts or even more.

Even though women are less likely than men to drive after drinking and therefore to be involved in fatal alcohol-related car accidents, women have a higher relative risk of driver fatality than men at similar blood alcohol concentrations. That is, they are more likely to have a fatal road accident than a male with the same alcohol levels. Some studies which have found differences in how alcohol affects the performance of males and females when it comes to driving tasks may help to explain this.

Of course, we need to remember that everyone is different and there are always going to be exceptions to the rule, but on average, women achieve higher concentrations of alcohol in the blood and become more impaired than men after drinking the same amount of alcohol.

The public consumption of alcohol by women is a fairly new phenomenon. Women weren't allowed in public bars in Australia until relatively recently, and now research is indicating that the group of people in our society that are showing the greatest increase in rates of drinking are young women.

It is really no surprise that this is occurring. New products specifically designed for the female market, such as the 'ready-to-drinks' (RTDs), have become increasingly popular with this group. For a long time, the barrier to young women drinking was the taste. Alcoholic drinks can be difficult for the young palate to become accustomed to, particularly the strong-tasting spirits such as rum and whisky. With alcohol companies now adding carbonated, sugary soft drink to the mix, that barrier has well and truly been blown away.

Females are also now a key target as far as advertising and marketing is concerned. If I go back to my teenage years I remember that every alcohol advertisement on TV involved a bunch of 'Aussie blokes' riding horses and climbing mountains. In those days, advertising was targeting men in their late twenties and early thirties, and the key product they were pushing was beer. Nowadays, the female market is considered a growth area as far as profits are concerned.

If you have a daughter it is important she knows that the risks around alcohol are greater for her than for her male friends. Make sure she knows not to try to keep up with her boyfriend or male siblings or friends, and dissuade girls from buying drinks in rounds when there are males in the group.

• What is a standard drink and why is it important?

We hear more and more about standard drinks these days. A 'standard drink' is any drink containing 10 grams of alcohol. One standard drink always contains the same amount of alcohol, regardless of the container size or alcohol type, whether it be beer, wine or a spirit. It is basically a unit of measurement, designed to measure the amount of alcohol consumed.

Instead of counting glasses or containers, drinkers are encouraged to count standard drinks as a much more reliable way of keeping track of how much alcohol they consume, as different containers hold varying amounts of alcohol. In Australia, the number of standard drinks in alcohol is always shown on the label of the container.

A great deal of time is dedicated to teaching young people about standard drinks during school-based drug education lessons dealing with alcohol. Without a doubt most young people have heard about the concept of standard drinks, but how do they really use them?

If I asked you as a parent how you used standard drinks, I could pretty well guarantee that the only way you do would be in relation to driving—that is, how many drinks can you have and still be under the limit? It would be great to hear that most of you actually used them to drink at levels recommended by health authorities, but I very much doubt it!

For most young people, particularly those who are high-risk drinkers, the only use they have for standard drinks is to work out which container of alcohol will get them drunk fastest. Most teenagers have no use for them in relation to driving. Many of them are unable to drive and those that do have licences are not allowed to drive with any alcohol in their systems, so the concept of a standard drink becomes superfluous.

So am I suggesting we scrap the whole standard drink idea? Absolutely not—but I think it is important to recognise that the concept means very little to our young people and has no real use until later in their life, particularly in regard to driving. Even then, there are very few people who use them to ensure that they drink at healthy levels. It needs to be remembered too that the whole concept of counting anything when you're drinking, whether it be cans or bottles or standard drinks, is extremely difficult and fraught with problems.

• Can you really overdose on alcohol?

We talk so much about illegal drugs like heroin that we often forget that legal drugs such as alcohol cause just as many problems, if not more. One of those problems is overdose.

Overdose means exactly what it says—it occurs when you take 'over the dose', or too much of a substance. We tend to think of overdose as meaning that someone has died—what we know as a 'fatal overdose'—but that is not always the case. Most overdoses do not result in someone's death.

Alcohol, like any other drug taken in large amounts, can lead to an overdose situation. Binge drinking or 'drinking to get drunk' is often the cause for alcohol poisoning. When someone drinks alcohol faster than their liver can metabolise it, the amount of alcohol in the blood rises, sometimes to a danger point. This can lead to an overdose situation. At very high blood alcohol levels, a person loses consciousness and goes into a coma. People do die as a result of alcohol poisoning.

When you hear about someone dying from 'alcohol poisoning' it usually means the person has died in one of three ways. The first indicates that the blood alcohol level was so high that the depressant effects of the drug slowed down the parts of the brain and nervous system that control breathing and the heart. Usually the drinker dies because he or she has stopped breathing and the heart has stopped, usually while unconscious.

I was called to a school due to an alcohol-related incident on a school camp. The year ten class had gone to a camp about a two-hour drive from the city. One boy had decided to smuggle a bottle of whisky along. Strangely, he had elected not to drink the whisky while they were away, but instead pulled out the bottle on the bus ride back to school.

Sitting in the back of the bus with four or five of his friends, he decided to play a skolling game. We don't know the whole story, but we do know that he lost two successive rounds. As a result he had to skol two neat glasses of whisky. The young boy became quite sick and passed out. The rest of the boys ignored him, considering him to be pretty pathetic, passing out after just two glasses.

When they got back to school the teacher ushered the students off the bus. It was then that he noticed the boy lying on the back seat. He asked one of the boy's friends what was wrong, and was told that the boy was asleep.

The teacher walked to the back of the bus and tried to wake the young man up but he couldn't—the boy was dead.

The second type of death is one that we unfortunately hear of more and more. While unconscious, the drinker has been sick and choked on his or her own vomit. There are also rare reports of an unconscious drinker choking on his or her own tongue.

Belinda finally convinced her parents to let her have a sixteenth birthday party. She didn't want an open house; all she wanted was to have a few of her girlfriends around for a sleepover. There was one more request—she and her friends wanted to drink alcohol. After much deliberation (and a great deal of soul-searching) by her parents, they agreed to allow a small amount of alcohol to be served, as long as the parents of the other girls gave their permission.

After permission was granted, Belinda's parents bought two four-packs of pre-mixed spirits to be drunk between the six girls on the night of the party. With each bottle measuring just over one standard drink, that meant each girl would be drinking about 1.5 standard drinks, an amount Belinda's parents believed could not cause too much harm.

Unfortunately, the girls thought exactly the same thing. They had managed to find someone to buy extra alcohol and hid it around the house before the party got started. The party was being held in the back room, while Belinda's parents stayed in the front room, away from the action. With no adult supervision the girls started to drink . . . and drink . . . and drink . . .

As she was the birthday girl, Belinda drank quite a lot more than any of the other girls. In fact, she drank to the point where she passed out. Her friends immediately swung into action. They knew they should do something to keep her safe but unfortunately they were drunk and they got it all wrong.

Of course, what they should have done was call Belinda's parents, just a room away. However, the girls were scared; they had broken the rules by bringing extra alcohol to the party. They were afraid of getting into trouble so decided to look after Belinda themselves. They had been taught that it is important to put someone into the recovery position, so that is what they did.

They picked Belinda up and put her into the recovery position on her side on a leather couch. However, instead of having her face the front, they put her facing the back of the couch. While she was lying down and unconscious, Belinda vomited. As it was a leather couch, the vomit lay in a pool and was not absorbed into the fabric. When she was sick, Belinda convulsed and her head rolled into the pool and she drowned in her own vomit.

Amazingly the girls did not leave Belinda's side and had no idea that she had died. As she was facing the back of the couch, music was playing and they were all intoxicated, they did not notice that she had vomited or that her head had rolled into a dangerous position. It was about twenty minutes before they discovered that their friend was dead.

Finally, the alcohol could react with another drug that the person has taken and cause death. This can occur with a prescription drug, an over-the-counter medication or an illegal substance. These deaths are even more unpredictable than the first two types as they can happen even if the person has not drunk a great deal.

The most tragic thing about the two cases I've cited above is that neither of those two young people should have died. If one of their friends with them at the time had known what to do, they would still be alive today. No one need die from alcohol poisoning. If those who have overdosed receive medical assistance and are given help to breathe until the alcohol's effects have worn off, they will survive.

Unfortunately one of the most common responses to alcohol poisoning is to put the person to bed to 'let them sleep it off'. Over the years I have been involved with a number of cases where young people have been put to bed and were found dead the next morning. It is important to note here that this does not just happen to young people—adults can die in exactly the same way.

I work with a number of sports groups across the country and know of a death that occurred several years ago while a team was travelling overseas. They had just had a major win and were celebrating as many sporting teams do—with lots of alcohol.

When most of the party returned to the team's hotel, a small group of the guys decided to kick on. They went to another bar and kept drinking. Eventually one of the blokes from the team's management collapsed in a drunken stupor. Taking this as a sign to call it a night, the rest of them picked up their mate and carried him back to the hotel. They took him to his room, dropped him on his bed and left him there.

The next morning he didn't show up for breakfast or for the training session that followed. Calls to his room met with no response. Now more than a little concerned, team officials got the hotel staff to let them into his room. He was exactly where his drinking partners had left him, lying face up on the bed—he had vomited in the night and choked on his own vomit.

An important message to take away from this story is never to put a drunk person to bed without monitoring them carefully. If they do appear to be sober enough to leave alone, make sure they are in a safe position (the 'recovery position'), lying on their side with their head tilted slightly to help them to breathe more effectively. Put a pillow behind them to prevent them from rolling onto their back during the night.

Although drinking to the point of drunkenness is seen as 'just something that you do', an alcohol overdose is very dangerous and it is extremely important that the person affected is looked after. So how do you know if a person is just drunk or suffering from alcohol poisoning? If you see any one of the following signs, you should seek medical help immediately—this is not something you can deal with alone.

- The person is unconscious and can't be awakened by pinching, prodding or shouting.
- The skin is cold, clammy, pale or bluish or purplish in colour, indicating they are not getting enough oxygen.
- The person is breathing very slowly. If there are more than ten seconds between breaths, this is an emergency.
- The person vomits without waking up.

Remember, people do die from alcohol poisoning. Although alcohol is often seen as a harmless bit of fun, things can go wrong and alcohol poisoning or overdose is a real risk if people drink too much, too quickly.

• How do you get rid of a hangover?

At some stage in their lives, many Australians have experienced waking up the morning after a big night to a spinning room, a violent headache and a rush to the bathroom. Unfortunately, it would appear that this is also a regular occurrence for some of our young people. But what causes a hangover?

The simple answer is, of course, drinking too much alcohol. A hangover is the result of your body experiencing a mild reaction resulting from an overdose of alcohol and certain toxins that are associated with alcohol consumption. Your body attempts to protect itself by producing enzymes to break down and remove the toxins from your body. However, the process does not occur fast enough and the resulting build-up of toxins in your body is believed to be a major cause of hangovers. When the toxin level exceeds your body's ability to metabolise them in an efficient manner, you experience the unpleasant and classic symptoms of a hangover described above.

Another major cause of a hangover is dehydration. Difficult to believe, particularly when you see how much some people can drink, but as you are drinking alcohol, your body is actually losing fluid. This is due to the diuretic effect of alcohol. Ever noticed how much you urinate when you drink alcohol? While you are losing more fluids than usual, you are also losing important vitamins and nutrients. It is not known how much dehydration contributes to a hangover, but most experts believe it plays a pretty big role, and all agree that at the very least it's going to exacerbate the symptoms.

Congeners are also believed to contribute to a hangover, particularly in relation to the headache you may experience the morning after. Congeners are toxic chemicals and impurities that are formed during the fermentation process used to make alcohol, with some forms of alcohol having more of them than others. The rule of thumb here is the clearer your drink, the fewer problems you will have the next morning. This is why many people believe that white wines and spirits such as vodka cause fewer hangovers.

Another factor to consider is alcohol's effect on your quality of sleep. If you haven't slept well it's likely to make you feel even more grumpy and tired than you would anyway. When you fall asleep after a big night of drinking, the high levels of alcohol in your system prevent your brain from performing some of its routine tasks, such as managing your sleep pattern. As a result, you're unable to enter the important REM (Rapid Eye Movement) or dreaming stage of sleep, which is essential if you want a really good night's rest. Thus apart from toxins, dehydration and congeners, a lack of proper rest is going to add to your discomfort.

So are there any ways to get rid of a hangover?

Although there are many commercial remedies, as well as a whole pile of old wives' tales, the truth is that there is only one cure—time!

One of those old wives' tales is 'a hair of the dog that bit you'. This remedy recommends having a drink the next morning to relieve the effects of alcohol consumed the night before. The hangover victim is supposed to drink the same drink that they drank the night before, although often the preferred beverage is a Bloody Mary. To a point, this may actually be effective. When you wake up with a hangover your body is going through mild withdrawal from an alcohol overdose. Having more alcohol may alleviate some symptoms of the hangover (and a drink like a Bloody Mary contains vitamins your body may be craving), but the effects are only temporary. At some time or another you are going to have to face the hangover—and you might as well get it over with quickly.

So if you can't get rid of it, how about trying to prevent one from occurring? After all, prevention is better than cure. Of course, the best way to prevent a hangover is not to drink too much, but failing that here are a few guidelines that will make drinking safer for you and your teenager, should they choose to drink:

- Before you go out, eat a good meal. Eating pasta or other carbohydrate-rich foods will fuel the body in preparation for a big night. It will also slow the absorption of alcohol into the bloodstream, preventing you getting drunk too fast.
- Make sure the first drink you consume is water or non-alcoholic. You will drink the first drink of the evening much faster than any other if you are thirsty. Use a non-alcoholic drink to quench that thirst.
- Try to rehydrate before you go to bed. Make sure you drink water throughout the evening to space the amount of alcohol

you drink, but a couple of glasses before you go to sleep should help prevent the dehydrating effect of alcohol.

• What does it mean if I don't remember things when I drink?

Sometimes we don't bother to give our young people information because we believe it's too obvious. It's just common sense, we reason. But as I've learnt over the years, that's not always the case.

I couldn't even tell you how many times I have been asked by students, mostly young women, about 'blackouts'. Usually the question goes something like: 'What does it mean if, after drinking a bit, I can't remember what happened the night before?' That this question is asked by so many young people quite clearly shows that they don't know nearly as much as they—or we—think they do.

I still remember the first time I was asked this question, by a girl in the front row of the audience. I asked her to give me a little more information. Did she mean large pieces of the evening or a few minutes, and how much was she drinking when this happened? Her answer floored me—it was usually hours at a time that were lost and she was averaging about six to eight ready-to-drinks every time she drank. This young girl had been extremely fortunate; to her knowledge, nothing bad had happened to her during these memory lapses—but how long was her luck going to hold out?

Jessica was sixteen years old. When I met her she had been drinking regularly for two to three years. She went out every Saturday night with her friends and had never had a significant problem with her drinking until a couple of months before I visited her school.

She had gone out for what she considered a 'fun night'. She and her friends had pooled their resources and bought a bottle of vodka to share. At some point during the evening, Jessica became separated from her friends. Instead of going home straightaway, instead of calling her mother on her mobile to come and pick her up, instead of making a sensible decision, Jessica decided to stay at the party and continue to drink. Everything was fine until she blacked out.

She remembers nothing until she woke up the next morning in a strange house, in a strange bed, without any underwear on. She got up and moved through the now-empty house. She finally found a phone and next to it were a number of envelopes which all had the same address on them. She quite cleverly worked out that this must be where she was and called a friend to come and pick her up.

When her friend arrived a while later she immediately took Jessica to the emergency department of the local hospital. The staff quickly realised that she needed specialist attention and escorted her to the sexual assault unit where she was assigned a counsellor. An examination was conducted and, when she was given the results some time later—and I need to reiterate that she had no memory of the evening whatsoever—she discovered that she had been sexually assaulted.

Stories involving drinking to excess and sexual assault are not uncommon. A number of young women have told me their stories over the years, each one of them asking me to share their experience with other young people around the country so that others could avoid enduring a similar trauma.

This was never more true than with Libby. This young lady was one of the bravest young women I have ever met and her story illustrates clearly how one night of drinking to excess can change your life forever.

Libby was fifteen years old and had been dating her boyfriend, Paul, for three months. He was two years older than her and went to the same school in a small country town. As was the norm for a Saturday night, they both went to the 'big party' that was taking place. It was being held just outside town at a home where there were going to be no adults present, and 'everyone' was going to be there.

When they got to the party they both started drinking. One of Paul's best mates was driving so there were no worries about getting home safely. Libby, as usual, drank to excess, and it wasn't too long before she was well and truly intoxicated. Then she had a blackout. When she recovered she found herself in the middle of a conversation that appeared totally normal. She had not passed out, she just couldn't remember anything that had happened in the previous three hours.

Libby regularly experienced blackouts; sometimes they lasted for a few seconds, sometimes for minutes and occasionally for an hour or more. Her friends would often talk about something that she had done during the night of which she had no recollection. She didn't really worry about them: she believed blackouts were just something that happened when you drank alcohol. She doesn't have much of a memory of the rest of that Saturday night. She had drunk too much and just wanted to go home.

At school on Monday everything appeared relatively normal, although Libby began to feel that something was going on that she wasn't privy to. A number of the girls at school were whispering together and when she asked what it was about she was met with silence. It wasn't until the Wednesday that Libby found out what everyone else knew.

During her blackout on Saturday night Libby had lost her virginity to her boyfriend. Someone at the party had videoed her having sex on a mobile phone and had subsequently posted it on the internet. It wasn't long before most of the school knew about the video and it quickly became the talk of the town. When Libby and her family found out about it they were able to get the offending video taken off the site on which it had been posted, but by that time it was too late. Many people had already downloaded it, saving it onto their own computers where it would be available forever.

I have been using Libby's story in schools for some time now and it helps to show the real risks that young people face when they drink to excess. Unfortunately, the major problem with blackouts is that young people regard them as part of the alcohol experience, because no one has ever told them otherwise. When Libby related her story, she said that she had never given her previous blackouts a thought. Her friends all experienced them to some degree, or at least they said they did, and Libby just didn't know any different.

When young people are informed that blackouts and memory lapses are *not* 'normal' and usually only occur when you have drunk far too much, they are often very surprised. I have no evidence to show that giving this information to the young people I come in contact with changes their behaviour, but at least they are informed and they know the risk they are taking.

Without doubt we talk about this area of blackouts far more often in relation to young women, mainly due to the risk of sexual assault, but it is important to remember that young men can experience harm in this way too.

After hearing my stories about young women and sexual assault during a school presentation one day, a year ten boy named Dean approached me to share his story. He was concerned that I had not raised the issue of young men risking harm when they drank to excess.

Dean, who lived in a beachside suburb of a major city, had gone out with his mates and spent the evening drinking beer. The gang of friends were on a beach and, although Dean hadn't had too much to drink at this stage, he successfully pushed himself well and truly over the edge when his friends dared him to skol a large soft-drink bottle full of some spirit mix. He emptied the bottle and remembers little that occurred after that.

From what the police were able to piece together in the days after the event, Dean had apparently become quite abusive towards his mates and finally pulled away from the group. An hour later he was seen by another group of young people at another beach, this time shouting out abuse at passers by.

No one knows anything about the next few hours. It was not until the following morning that Dean's parents were woken by a knock at their front door. When they opened it they found their son lying on the verandah, covered in blood. He was naked apart from a pair of undies, and had been bashed and robbed. Money, clothing and all his personal belongings had been stolen.

Drinking to excess exposes you to a number of risks. Not remembering what happened the night before should be explained to a young person as a warning sign that they are drinking too much. Letting your child know that there are people in this world who may take advantage of this type of situation, whether your child is male or female, is also extremely important. Sexual assault and robbery are just two of the possible outcomes.

• Is the story about 'breaking the seal' true? Once I've gone to the toilet during the night is that it—I won't be able to stop?

Over the years I've heard a number of different definitions of 'breaking the seal'. For both young men and women, it is usually the belief that you 'break the seal' when you first urinate after you have been drinking alcohol, causing you to have to go to the toilet every ten or fifteen minutes thereafter. (There is also a belief among a core group of high-risk drinking young men that the same principle applies with vomiting during a drinking game or serious drinking session.)

Naomi and her friends enjoyed a night out and none of them drank to excess. However, one night Naomi found herself in a highly embarrassing situation after drinking.

They had all heard of 'breaking the seal' and since they did not want to go back and forth to the toilet all evening, they tried to delay their first visit for as long as they could. The trick, they believed, was to hold on for as long as possible—even if it was painful.

Naomi had been partying for a couple of hours and had wanted to go to the toilet for some time, but they were about to travel across town to the next party and she was sure she could make it. But when she got into her friend's car and relaxed, the floodgates opened—literally! Not only did she wet herself but she managed to wet much of the back seat, as well as some of her friends.

As embarrassing as this situation is, it's an instructive one; when your body tells you to urinate or vomit, it is usually doing so for a reason. Trying to stop yourself is not only foolish, it could be dangerous.

So why are you able to hold the first few drinks with little problem and after that experience so much difficulty? Have you done something to your bladder, have you broken some magical 'seal'?

Quite the contrary. Essentially, it has to do with the rising level of alcohol in your bloodstream. After your first couple of drinks your blood alcohol level is still relatively low. However, after that it starts to rise steeply, particularly if you are drinking quickly. Alcohol is a diuretic and affects the hormone that helps your body hold onto water. As a result, the amount of urine you produce increases out of proportion to the amount you drink, and your bladder fills up faster and faster. This is why you get dehydrated despite the fact that you are taking in fluids.

• Should I let my child go to Schoolies Week and is it really as bad as the media paints it?

Schoolies Week has been around in one form or another for a long time. When I finished high school I can remember a range of things that some of my classmates did in the weeks following the last day of exams. Some of them were illegal, others extremely dangerous and the rest just plain stupid.

Since that time, and particularly over the last decade, Schoolies Week, as it has become known, has become bigger and more commercialised and received much more media attention. As a result there is increasing social pressure on young people leaving school to attend Schoolies Week celebrations in one form or another.

Community interest has risen also and you can pretty well guarantee that every year crews of TV reporters will descend on the Gold Coast to try to capture the most sensational footage. Without fail they usually manage to find some young people who agree to be interviewed on national television and talk about their alcohol- (or, even better, drug-) fuelled week at Schoolies, thus reinforcing many parents' belief that it is out of control and without merit.

One of the best things about all the attention is that the promoters of Schoolies events have been forced to up the ante in terms of organisation and must now do their very best to provide a safe environment for the young people attending. You only have to type *Schoolies* into an internet search engine and it will return hundreds of sites dedicated to providing information to young people and their parents about the events and how to keep safe.

The whole concept behind Schoolies Week is to give young people who have been studying for the past twelve years the opportunity to let their hair down after their final exams. When you think about it, whoever planned secondary school didn't put a lot of thought into it; at the same time as they leave school, kids learn to drive a car and are legally allowed to start drinking—not a particularly healthy combination!

Over the years I have attended a number of Schoolies Week celebrations and although there have always been incidents, usually linked to excessive alcohol consumption, for the most part I have found the young people to be well behaved and reasonably sensible.

The most concerning aspect of the event is the social pressure on young people attending Schoolies to behave in a certain way. There is an expectation from very early on that all the teenagers going to Schoolies will drink to excess and, as a result, behave badly. The media does a great job of convincing young people that this is the type of behaviour expected of them and, unfortunately, many of them try to live up to it.

Stephen was seventeen years old when he attended Schoolies Week celebrations on the Gold Coast. He was not a big drinker but usually had a couple of beers on a Saturday night when he went to parties in the small country town he lived in.

He and three of his mates had rented an apartment for the week and were well prepared for a week of partying. On the drive up to the Gold Coast, they had spent up big on alcohol—over $1000 on a selection of spirits and beer. None of them had money to burn but they thought that this would last them for the week, with some to spare.

On the first day they met up with a few other friends and invited them over for some drinks before they went to an organised event. That ended up being a costly mistake. What was meant to be a small get-together ended up being a free-for-all, with gatecrashers arriving within the first hour. They not only took all the alcohol, they also stole many of the boys' personal belongings. The whole party lasted just over 90 minutes before the police were called.

I met Stephen the year after this had occurred. He was volunteering at Schoolies Week this time, and told me that he had learnt one of the most valuable lessons of his life from that event. On reflection, he realised that he and his mates were trying to do what they thought people at Schoolies Week *should* do, not what they were actually comfortable doing. Spending over $1000 on alcohol made no sense to him now, and trying to hold a party when you didn't know what you were doing was very risky.

It is important to remember that trying to prevent your son or daughter from attending this type of event could damage the relationship you have with them. Young people attending Schoolies are not in their early teens; they are usually very close to the legal drinking age or, in some cases, have already turned eighteen. They are at an age where they are going to have to make decisions on their own, and trying to prevent them from doing so is not recommended.

Regardless of that, you are still the parent and you are still allowed to voice your concerns about what they are doing and the risks they may encounter. That part of being a parent is never going to stop and you wouldn't be doing your job if you didn't do it.

My advice is to take a moment to sit down with your child and talk through the concerns you have. Then, after you have finished, give them the opportunity to explain how they intend to deal with the potential problems you have raised. What many parents discover during conversations like this is that we have a generation of young people to be proud of, with many of them doing their very best to look after themselves and their friends.

Every time you have a conversation with your child about risky behaviour it needs to end with a reinforcement of the message that you can be called at any time. It doesn't matter what they have done, you love them unconditionally and you will be there for them. There may be consequences, but that's down the track; all that's important in that moment is that they are safe and know that you love them.

One of the saddest things I have ever heard come from a young person's mouth was at the first Schoolies Week I ever attended. A young girl, heavily intoxicated and having difficulty breathing, had been brought to the medical tent. She was barely conscious and had been found alone in the street. When we asked if there was someone we could call to be with her, her response was a very timid 'Not my mum!'

3
LOOKING AFTER YOUR FRIENDS

After speaking to tens of thousands of students over the last decade or so, it still never ceases to amaze me how much the young people of today want to look after each other. When I think back to my peer group in adolescence I am sure we were very similar—during the teenage years, your friends can become your second family, supporting you through this very difficult and emotional time. That said, I am increasingly impressed by the care, compassion and empathy that most of today's kids exhibit.

I have already said that the vast majority of questions I get asked by school students focus on issues around personal safety and how to look after their friends. This chapter examines some of those questions.

I urge parents to read this section carefully and ask yourself how these questions relate to the information you have been giving your child. I assure you, you would be a very unusual parent if they even come close to matching up. In all my years of giving presentations I have yet to meet a parent who has provided information to their child on the topic I get asked about more frequently in schools than any other: 'How do I look after a drunk friend?'

There are parents who will look at some of these questions and be concerned that by addressing them with their child they might be seen to be condoning their use of alcohol or tacitly encouraging risky behaviour.

Of course you don't want to normalise risky behaviour, so how you present this sort of information is of paramount importance. To sit down with your child and give them instructions on how to look after a drunk friend does not provide a context, and could be dangerous. If, however, a conversation starts about alcohol and there is a discussion about responsible drinking, it would be entirely appropriate to provide information to your child about what to do should something go wrong.

Time and time again I have met young people who have lost friends simply because they did not know how to respond appropriately. Parents and teachers often say that 'young people know more than we do'—absolute garbage! Sometimes kids think they know more than us, but usually all they really want is information that is going to be useful to them: some helpful tips that they regard as credible and that have some meaning in their lives. So much of what they are taught in schools has very little relevance to their day-to-day lives and, when it comes to alcohol and other drug information, spewing out the short- and long-term effects of using various drugs is neither interesting nor relevant to most young people.

I guarantee that if you use some of the questions in this chapter as conversation starters, and you are honest and open with your child during the ensuing discussion, at the very least, your credibility rating will go through the roof!

This is the information your child wants to know. It doesn't matter whether they drink or don't drink, whether they use drugs or don't use drugs, if it is delivered in the right way, in the appropriate context, you will see your child take this information, absorb it, share it with others and use it in the future.

• How do you look after someone who has drunk too much?

Not too long ago I was asked to give a series of presentations to a private girls' school. I was to talk to the year tens, elevens and twelves over the period of a day. I began with the youngest group and, after my talk, invited questions. By the time four or five questions had been asked I could see a pattern—they were all about how to look after someone who was drunk. I stopped the questions and asked the girls to indicate how many of them had recently had to look after a drunk friend. Within this group of fifteen-year-old girls, over 50 per cent put up their hands.

When the next two groups came through later in the day, I began my presentation by asking them the same question. Over 70 per cent of the year elevens and almost the entire year twelve group had at one time or another needed to look after an intoxicated friend.

When asked what they had actually done in these situations, there were a wide range of responses. When asked why they had responded in a particular way—had they been given some instruction or advice by someone, for example?—almost all of them said that they had been given no information, suggesting instead that their 'maternal instincts had kicked in'.

My first dealing with Matt was when I received a phone call from him asking me to present to a group of his friends on the topic of 'looking after your mates'.

Matt was fifteen at the time and had recently been witness to a life-threatening incident involving one of his friends and alcohol. A group of them had gone to a party and, although some of them had previously experimented with alcohol, they were all fairly naïve. One of Matt's friends drank far too much and started to become very sick. He was vomiting and they were having a lot of trouble keeping him awake. None of the boys wanted to call for help for fear of getting into trouble with the police or, even worse, their parents. For almost two hours, Matt and two others nursed their drunken friend, praying that he would come around and be okay.

Luck was on Matt's side that night and his friend survived, apparently no worse for wear. However, the evening had a tremendous impact on Matt. He could not believe that he had been put into that position without any information. He spoke to teachers at his school and asked why they hadn't been given any lessons on how to look after someone who was drunk.

Unfortunately, Matt was met with brick walls at his school. He was given some very flippant answers, basically telling him that they shouldn't have been drinking anyway and that it was not the school's job to 'babysit' on the weekends.

Far from being discouraged, Matt called a number of people (me included) and set about putting together a 'survival course' for his peers. He involved the Ambulance Service, a local GP and a range of other people, asking them to provide information and skills to prepare young people to handle the risks associated with excessive drinking.

Matt is now in his early twenties and has gone from strength to strength. The course he created was adopted by his school and he remains actively involved in providing information to young people on a range of issues.

Matt is just one example of the amazing young people I have come in contact with over the years who are rarely acknowledged in our community. Not all young people have the same drive or passion as Matt, however all young people (I believe without exception) want to know how to look after themselves and their friends.

So how *do* you look after someone who has drunk too much? On pages 64–68 we discuss overdose situations and how to tell the difference between someone who is drunk and someone who is poisoned, but for now let's look at someone who is drunk and can be looked after by friends.

There are a number of simple messages that all young people, whether they are drinkers or non-drinkers, should know when it comes to looking after friends who have had too much to drink:

- Stick with them and never leave them alone.
- Monitor them.

- Reassure them.
- Keep them comfortable.
- Keep them hydrated.
- If in doubt, call for help.

The most important message here is to make sure you stick with a drunk friend and never leave them alone. Years ago there was a government campaign called 'How Will You Feel Tomorrow?' that showed a young woman alone in a toilet cubicle, vomiting. Being alone in a cubicle vomiting is incredibly dangerous. If the person passes out and they've locked the door, how is help going to get in? Never, ever let someone go to the toilet, or anywhere else for that matter, to be sick alone.

Monitor your friend carefully. The line between being drunk and being poisoned can be fine. If they are already unwell and drank more alcohol in the past hour or so, there is every likelihood that they could become worse.

When you are unwell after drinking it can be very frightening. Adding to the discomfort is the fear that their parents may discover what they have been up to or that the police may become involved. Friends being close, reassuring them that everything will be okay, is important.

If they are feeling sick there is every likelihood that they may be feverish. Their temperature may rise and often they will want to take off surplus clothing and footwear. Putting a cold compress (or even a cold water bottle) on the back of the person's neck can make them feel much more comfortable. Make sure that there is also something warm to wrap around them just in case they start to get cold—particularly true in situations where young people have gathered in parks or country areas to drink.

Hydration is a difficult one. If they are not being sick, make sure that your friend replaces lost fluids. That is, if they have been urinating a lot, they need to drink water. It is also important to make sure that someone is hydrated if they are vomiting, but if you give them water to drink during that time, it is highly likely that they will simply vomit it back up relatively quickly. A piece of advice that I give young people is to soak a T-shirt or cloth in cold water and then have the person vomiting suck on that between bouts. That way they are rehydrating and also making their mouth feel a little more pleasant, but not gulping down water that is likely to make them vomit more.

If in doubt, don't hesitate to call for medical assistance. It's hard to be too specific here as it's not always easy to say what constitutes a 'medical emergency'. Young people need to know that they won't get in trouble for calling an ambulance. Even if the ambulance arrives and the situation has resolved itself, it's better to be safe than sorry. They also need to know that as a general rule, the police will not attend a medical emergency involving alcohol or other drugs unless another crime, such as violence, has taken place.

Dialling 000 can be a daunting experience when you first do it. I still remember my first time—I got the number wrong and called 911 (which will not get you connected to emergency services in Australia although some mobile phones sold in Australia will redirect such calls to 000)!

Running through making a 000 call with your teenager can be useful, just in case.

Justine lived in a country area and was out with her best friend Katy. Both were fifteen years old. They were at a party with a group of older boys and felt completely out of their depth. Most of the people were older and for the first time the girls were drinking straight spirits, not pre-mixed drinks.

Katy became unwell quite early and it was obvious that the boys they had arrived with were now completely uninterested in them both. When Katy lost consciousness and began to vomit without waking up, Justine knew it was a medical emergency and tried to get help.

The older girls at the party told Justine that Katy would be okay and to let her 'sleep it off'. Knowing the danger, Justine called 000. The operator asked, 'Which service do you require?', the standard first question for the 000 line. Justine, who was already scared and confused, had no idea what the operator meant and when the follow-up question asked whether she wanted 'police, fire or ambulance', she completely freaked out and hung up.

Fortunately, Justine finally worked up the courage to redial 000 and request an ambulance.

It's all well and good to tell our children to call 000, but they also need to know what happens next. (And they need to know that you support them in their decision to make this type of call.)

When you call 000 the operator will ask whether you need the police, fire or ambulance service. Depending on whether you use a mobile, fixed line, voice-over-internet-protocol (VoIP) service or a payphone, you may also be asked to provide details of the state and town you are calling from. The operator will then connect you to the emergency service organisation you have requested.

If you are calling from a landline, your location details will automatically appear on the operator's screen and will be passed on to the emergency service you request. However, you may still be asked by the operator (or the emergency service) to confirm your location.

However, we know that most young people will be using a mobile phone. Unfortunately, in these cases the operator will not be able to pinpoint the location. Mobile phone users should provide the operator with as much information as they can about the location of the emergency, including the state or territory and the town or suburb. This simple step will ensure that the emergency call is connected to the appropriate state or territory emergency service organisation.

It will be useful for you to discuss with your child the sort of questions the ambulance operator may ask them. These will most probably include the following:

- What is the exact address of the emergency? (The operator will ask for the suburb name and nearest cross street.)
- What is the phone number you are calling from? (This information is important in case the operations centre needs to call back to obtain further information.)
- What is the problem? Tell me exactly what happened.
- How old is the patient?
- Is s/he conscious?
- Is s/he breathing?

Once these questions have been answered an ambulance is sent. The person calling needs to remain calm, and not hang up until the operator has obtained all of the required information. There may be some additional questions asked or instructions given, depending on the situation.

One important message that we do not emphasise enough to our children is that they need to know the address of where they are partying. If something goes wrong, the 000 operator will need a location—if you don't know the street address this will prove difficult. This is a particular problem in country areas, where young people often hold parties in hard-to-reach places and at almost non-existent addresses. One really useful tip is to get your child into the habit of taking the address of the party they are attending on a slip of paper just in case. Start this early and you're unlikely to meet as much resistance.

It is also important to let your teenagers know that 112 is the international standard emergency number which can only be dialled on mobile phones. You can dial 112 anywhere in the world with mobile coverage and it will automatically default to that country's emergency number.

For those people who are deaf, or who have a hearing or speech impairment, there is also a text-based Emergency Call Service number—106. This service operates using a teletypewriter (TTY) but does not accept voice calls or SMS messages.

• Why do you vomit when you've drunk too much? Should you encourage vomiting and when should you seek medical help?

Many parents can remember a time in their past when they had a little bit too much to drink and found themselves doubled up and vomiting. It's not a particularly pleasant experience and most people only ever do it once—they never want to go back there.

Although many young people talk about wanting to get 'drunk' or 'wasted' when they go out with their friends, I have yet to speak to one who intentionally set out to make themselves sick.

Vomiting is an experience that almost all people, young and old, abhor. Yet every weekend, thousands of Australians drink to the point of throwing up. For some young people vomiting is perceived as just an unavoidable part of the 'alcohol experience'—a negative part, but a part nevertheless. Unfortunately, many are unaware that vomiting can be life-threatening.

Felicity was fifteen years old, and she and her best friend Thalia had gone out one Saturday night as they had many times before. As always, alcohol played a big part in the evening and both girls became quite drunk. Thalia began to feel extremely sick and told her friend that she was going to go outside to vomit. Felicity, being a good friend, went with her to the front garden of the party and sat with her. Holding her hair behind her head, patting her on her back and regularly providing her with sips of water, Felicity did what any friend would do.

This went on for some time. In fact it went on for so long that Thalia became quite embarrassed and urged her friend to go back inside and join the party. At first Felicity refused, but finally Thalia convinced her. She was feeling better, she told her friend, she just needed a bit of air and then she would follow her in. Felicity was still unsure but she did want to go back to the party, so she went inside. What could go wrong? Her friend was sitting on the front lawn of a house in the suburbs, it was well lit and there were lots of people around.

Unfortunately, Thalia was still severely affected by alcohol and, not long after she was left alone, she passed out on the lawn. She landed awkwardly, her chin hitting her chest, and then vomited. Within seconds the vomit had blocked her airway and she had choked to death.

Alcohol is a powerful depressant and can cause death directly by 'turning off' the brain areas that control consciousness, respiration and heart rate, resulting in unconsciousness, coma and then death.

In many cases, drinking too much alcohol will make you sick and you will stop drinking. There are many old wives' tales about why someone vomits after drinking, but the real reason is quite simple—you've been poisoned. Your brain actually has specialised poison-control cells that detect when you have had too much alcohol and send a signal to your stomach to vomit. Vomiting is an attempt to get rid of any unabsorbed alcohol. If you can prevent any alcohol that's still in the stomach from being absorbed into the bloodstream, it may prevent further poisoning and, in the process, save your life.

Many young people try to encourage their friends to vomit in an attempt to sober them up. They may do this in a number of ways, including urging the person to stick their fingers down their throat, making them eat and making them drink copious amounts of water. Of course, vomiting is going to have no effect on the sobriety of the young person—all it will do is empty the contents of their stomach, possibly making them feel less nauseous. However, it may be useful in preventing further alcohol from being absorbed and therefore reducing the risk of further poisoning. If someone feels as though they want to vomit they should never be discouraged from doing so.

Force-feeding someone or making them drink huge quantities of water is potentially dangerous, yet these are ways of 'looking after' friends that many kids try. Young people need to be aware that vomiting can be life-threatening. If someone is vomiting, or looks as though they may start, stick with them—never leave them, not even for a few seconds. It can take just seconds for someone to choke on their own vomit. Most of the time, you can look after someone who is vomiting just by being there and monitoring the person. However, there are times when you will need to call for help. Some of the warning signs to look out for include:

- vomiting for longer than 24 hours
- blood or bile in the vomit
- severe abdominal pain
- headache and stiff neck
- signs of dehydration, such as dark yellow urine or crying without tears.

Many young people have seen blood in a friend's vomit and become concerned. This is usually caused by prolonged and vigorous retching which leads to a tear in the small blood vessels of the throat or the oesophagus. It can usually be seen as small red streaks. Occasionally, bleeding can be caused when the person vomiting bites their tongue or the inside of their mouth. Although these are minor injuries and unlikely to cause significant problems, it is difficult to know for sure that these are the causes for the blood without a medical evaluation. It is always better to err on the side of caution and seek medical assistance immediately if you see blood in the vomit.

• How can you help someone sober up?

The mythology that exists around this question is quite astounding. This book is full of stories about young people finding themselves or their friends in trouble after trying to accelerate the sobering-up process, but the fact is, the only thing that will help sober anyone up is time.

The two most popular sobering-up methods are drinking a strong cup of coffee and putting someone under a cold shower. Neither of these is effective and one of them has proven to be extremely dangerous. If you think about the logistics of taking a drunk person (who is likely to have little coordination and be unable to stand properly) into a bathroom (one of the most dangerous rooms in the house—hard floors, sharp edges and, possibly, a sheet of glass), the hazards become all too clear.

Hillary was a year ten girl. She and her friends were pretty heavy drinkers and were having a big Saturday night at a classmate's party. They decided to play shot games. After skolling a large number of drinks the world began to spin and Hillary remembers little else about the evening. According to the other partygoers, Hillary started to lose consciousness and, although her two friends were drunk as well, they swung into action, deciding to put her under a cold shower to sober her up a little.

They took the unconscious girl into the bathroom and turned the shower on. The shower was over a bath so they had to lift Hillary into the bath to get her under the water. The girls struggled to hold onto their friend, but Hillary fell backwards, straight through the glass shower screen. The glass shattered and slashed her back and arms.

When Hillary came to the next morning she found herself in hospital. She still has the scars from that night but feels no anger towards her two friends. She admits she would have done the same thing if she had been in their situation. She just wishes someone had told her that it was a potentially dangerous thing to do and that, most importantly, it doesn't work!

Drinking a strong cup of coffee to battle alcohol's effects is another popular 'remedy'. The theory behind it is that strong coffee will contain a high dose of caffeine, the stimulant properties of which will counteract the alcohol's depressant effect. To a point this may have some limited effect, particularly if you haven't drunk that much, but most likely all that will happen is that for a short time you will be a more wide awake and alert drunk. You will not sober up!

In recent years a number of new 'cures' have emerged. One that is of great concern is the practice of giving someone water to help them sober up. You may think that this sounds fairly sensible, since it is ensuring that the person is well hydrated, and I would agree with you if that is what these young people were doing. Unfortunately it is not. Rather, they are 'force-feeding' their drunk friends water, some of them even using a funnel to pour the water down their friends' throats. The logic they give for this is that drinking water 'dilutes the alcohol'. Now, I'm not too sure where these guys think the alcohol goes when we drink it, but we've got to start telling our children that our bodies are not cordial bottles! It's not like the alcohol is sitting at the bottom of our stomachs and then we pour water over the top at the end of the night. When someone is drunk, one part of the body has been well and truly affected—the brain. No amount of water you drink at the end of the night is going to sober you up.

I need to reiterate that a small amount of water is not going to be harmful, but the reports from some young people about the amount of water they are giving to their friends are deeply disturbing. The reason we should worry about this is a condition known as water intoxication.

Water intoxication (also known as water poisoning or internal drowning) can be fatal, and is caused by the normal balance of electrolytes in the body being pushed outside safe limits by too much water. Most water intoxication-related deaths have resulted either from water-drinking contests (in which individuals attempt to drink huge amounts in a very short time), after taking ecstasy, or after long bouts of hard exercise. Tragically, it would seem that some young people could be putting their friends at risk of this condition due to the large amounts of water they are using to try to sober them up.

It is imperative that you talk to your child, whether they drink or not, about alcohol and its effects. It is also important that you make them aware that there is no way to help someone sober up apart from time, and that many of the so-called remedies will do more harm than good.

• I think a friend of mine might be using drugs. What should I do?

Sometimes young people approach me because they are concerned about a friend who they believe may be experimenting with illicit drugs. On other occasions I have come in contact with teenagers who are extremely worried about a friend who they think is a regular drug user. These are difficult situations to manage as the young people are often very distressed, having been concerned about their friend for some time and not knowing where to turn for help.

Erin, a year ten student, approached me after a talk I had given at her school. She was obviously upset and found it difficult to share her story. It was obvious that she was also extremely concerned about any teachers overhearing.

She travelled by bus to school and had a travelling companion, a year eleven boy, who she was obviously fond of. A few months before she had observed her friend purchasing something she believed to be cannabis from another boy on the bus. She had not said anything to anyone since that time but had seen another couple of transactions occurring since.

Sobbing, Erin expressed her concerns for her friend. What would happen to him if he got busted? What would his parents say? Would he go to jail? She was also racked with guilt because she had not said anything and the dealing was still occurring on the bus, right in view of some very young students. Could her inaction lead to problems for other students?

This had obviously been playing on her mind for some time and my presentation had brought it all to the surface. Fortunately

I was able to convince her to talk to a school counsellor and the school responded to the claims.

Some young people face extremely complex problems with no parental assistance simply because their parents are unaware that there is an issue. Giving your child the opportunity to raise these issues in a non-confrontational and non-judgmental environment is important.

The concerns young people describe usually involve their friend doing one or more of the following:

- giving up activities he or she used to participate in, particularly things they used to do together
- taking risks, including sexual risks
- appearing to be experiencing a range of mental health problems, including depression, paranoia or suicidal thoughts
- constantly talking about drugs and drug use and appearing to become entrenched in the drug culture
- associating with a new group of friends who are known drug users
- getting in trouble with the law and not seeming to care about the consequences.

Coping with these types of situations can be a terrible burden for a young person. The most important thing to do at this point is to support them as much as possible. It can take a great deal of courage for a teenager to even broach this subject with an adult. As I've indicated, often they have lived with this problem for some time, and they need to feel that they have done the right thing in coming forward and that the trust they have put in you is not going to be broken. Some of the questions that may be going around their heads could include the following:

- What if I get my friend into trouble?
- What if I lose my friend over this?
- What if I don't do anything and something awful happens?

Most young people are afraid to discuss serious issues with their friends because they fear being rejected and losing their friendship. It is never going to be easy to tell a friend that you believe they have a problem. It is vital that we let the teenager know that they are doing the right thing coming to you and that friendship is all about doing whatever is best for the other person. If they aren't going to discuss the problem with their friend, the chances are that no one will. If their friend is getting into trouble with drugs, the next person who speaks to them about the topic could be a police officer or an emergency department worker. Intervening in an appropriate way could prevent problems in the future.

So once you have reassured the young person that they have done the right thing in coming forward, and you have supported them in that decision, what information can you give them?

First, it is important for them to know that they *can* make a difference. Sometimes, simply expressing their concern about a friend's drug use can make the friend examine their behaviour more closely and, as a result, make changes. However, whether or not the friend acts on the advice and accepts the offer of friendship is completely the friend's decision and responsibility. As the old saying goes, you can lead a horse to water but you can't make it drink—you can only do your best, and that needs to be made very clear to the young person at the outset.

It is important that any intervention is well thought out and planned. Before acting, the teenager needs to gather as much information as they can about the topic and find out where help is available should their friend need it. Making sure you have the phone number of the alcohol and other drug helpline in your state or territory can be extremely useful. A list of these can be found on my website (www.darta.net.au). Visiting the local community health centre and picking up some brochures regarding services in the local area can also be of assistance. This information is not necessarily going to be given to the drug-using friend when they first raise the issue, but it is vital that they have it on hand if ever a crisis situation occurs.

Here are some approaches to assist a young person when they speak to their friend. Talk these through with your teenager if they ask for your help and try to work out what would be best in their particular situation.

- Before any attempt is made to have a discussion with your friend, prepare a list of issues or incidents that have occurred that have led to this point. Make these as specific as possible and make sure you focus on how their drug-using behaviour has affected *you*, not other people. For example: *When you were stoned you became very paranoid and accused me of things that weren't true. You said them in front of other people. That hurt my feelings.*

- Make sure you get the timing right. Having a discussion with a friend about their drug use when they are intoxicated is not going to be particularly productive, so social situations such as parties are not the ideal time for these types of conversations. Choose a time when your friend is most likely to accept the information. For example, the message is much more likely to have an impact after something bad has happened, so keep an eye out for an opportunity to raise the issue.

- Have your conversation somewhere where you can talk without fear of being overheard or interrupted. Public places such as schools and coffee shops can be difficult because the number of people around may make the friend feel self-conscious. A discussion in a bedroom or somewhere else quiet is more likely to be effective.

- No matter how bad the situation is, ensure that you include some type of positive message in the discussion. This will remind your friend that the conversation comes from a place of care and concern rather than criticism and judgment. *You are a wonderful person and I care about you very much, but your drug use is changing you and that upsets me.*

- Rather than talk about how bad their behaviour is and how it is affecting other people, restrict your comments to what you feel and what you have experienced of your friend's behaviour. Try hard to avoid generalisations like 'Everyone is really worried about you', as this will only lead to your friend becoming defensive and demanding to know who 'everyone' is. *I'm really worried about you and I don't want anything bad to happen to you.*

- Be sure to distinguish between the person and the behaviour. Emphasise the fact that you still care about your friend but when they have been using a drug their behaviour changes, and that is what is causing the problem—remove the drug and the person will return. *You are one of my best friends but when you smoke dope you change and are no fun to be with. When you are stoned you become boring.*

- Although it can be extremely difficult, don't accuse or argue. There is every possibility that your friend may get angry and react in a negative way. They may even lash out and bring up things they don't like about you. This should be no surprise and you should be prepared for such a reaction. You need to remain calm and stay focused on what you are trying to do by expressing your concerns as honestly and clearly as possible. *I understand there are things that I do that may upset you, but for now I am very concerned about what is happening to you. Maybe we can talk about my faults later. I am worried about your drug use and what is happening to our friendship.*

There is no way of knowing how the friend will react to this type of conversation and it will be important for the young person to have a sounding board to discuss what happened.

Helping a friend with a drug issue is hard work and can be a very difficult experience for all concerned. Your teenager may feel it is their responsibility to get their friend to stop using drugs and that they are being a bad friend if they don't succeed in their endeavours. They might also be very frightened that if their friend continues to use there may be tragic consequences. This is definitely my experience in schools where teenagers have been exposed to information about the consequences of drug use and then worry themselves sick about a friend who they think may be using. In these cases it is very important for the teenagers to know that they are not responsible for their friend's drug use. They need to be reminded that ultimately it is up to the individual to make decisions that will affect their life and no one else can do that for them.

It may sound harsh, but the reality is that as hard as you may try to get someone to stop using drugs or seek professional help, sometimes it just isn't going to happen—no matter what you do. If this is a situation that your child finds him or herself in, then you need to do the following:

- Make sure your child gets some additional support from either a responsible adult or a trained professional. As much as their friend may need help, it is important to remember that your teenager has also been through a tough experience and may need help in this situation.
- Convince your child to limit the amount of time they spend with the friend. If the friend is continuing to use drugs, they are also putting others at risk of a range of harms, particularly the legal consequences associated with illicit drugs.

It is important to make sure that the adolescent who is concerned for their friend is supported as much as possible. You need to be sure that they do not place themselves in a dangerous situation in the future, whether it be physical, psychological or legal danger.

If they have taken the huge step of opening up to you, make sure that you acknowledge the trust that they obviously have in you. As far as possible, avoid betraying that trust. However, there will always be cases, particularly when you discover that a young person is at risk, where you will have no alternative but to tell others what you have learnt. The important thing to remember here is that if the adolescent has got to the point of telling someone about their fears, they have usually got to a point where they have realised that there is no turning back, and that this is a crisis situation.

• One of my friends drinks far too much. What can I do?

Drinking alcohol is very much a part of many teenagers' lives and how they learn to socialise and become young adults. Unfortunately, some of these young people will drink to excess and get themselves into trouble. When this happens to an individual on a regular basis it is not unusual for their friends to become concerned about their mate's health and wellbeing. The problem is that most of these young people have no idea where to go for help and advice.

Young people can worry about their friend's drinking for a variety of reasons. Some of the disturbing situations that young people have described to me have involved friends exhibiting one or more of the following behaviours:

- becoming aggressive and violent after drinking
- avoiding their friends in order to go and get drunk
- planning drinking in advance, hiding alcohol from their friends or drinking alone
- having 'blackouts'—that is, forgetting parts of the night while drinking and, while drunk, behaving in ways that are not in character
- despite having been hospitalised due to their drinking, not changing their behaviour after the experience
- having one of a range of social problems, including abuse of some sort, and drinking to escape or cope with these issues
- drinking and driving.

It's just a fact of life that for the most part young people would never consider talking to their parents about this issue. Teenagers are well aware that Mum and Dad are likely to frown upon their drinking behaviour and reason that if they raise the issue of a friend having a problem with alcohol it could open a whole can of worms. There is also the risk that you may contact the friend's parents, which raises many issues around trust.

Unfortunately, young people don't seem to feel comfortable approaching any other adults about this sensitive issue either. Research shows that there are very few sources of help and information that teenagers would be willing to utilise. There are a few that they are likely to believe (i.e. they think they will have accurate information), and these include doctors or telephone helplines, but unfortunately they tend not to access them. Instead, they rely on their friends, and this can be dangerous. When it comes to the complex issue of alcohol it can even have life-threatening consequences.

Year eleven students Leslie and Sian approached me after I had given a presentation that dealt with alcohol poisoning. They told me that during my talk they and their group of friends had been thinking about one of their peers who had only recently joined their circle. Veronica was a year younger than the rest of them and did not have the drinking experience that the others had. This had resulted in some pretty nasty experiences for the group of friends, but Leslie, who had introduced Veronica to the others, felt particularly responsible for the young girl.

It appeared to the girls that Veronica had an extremely low tolerance to alcohol. It seemed to take only a very small amount of alcohol to get her drunk. After only two or three drinks she was 'pretty out of it' and Leslie and Sian were very concerned that she seemed to be trying to keep up with the rest of the group in order to fit in, and not pacing herself as she should considering her limited experience.

An incident only a fortnight before had brought the situation to a crisis point. The group of friends was at a party and lots of alcohol was being consumed. Veronica had drunk three bottles of pre-mixed spirits very quickly and became violently ill. Her friends had responded with care and concern as they usually did, though they were all getting a bit tired of looking after the young girl every Saturday night. They sat with her and tried to talk her through her drunken stupor, but this was not like the other nights—Veronica was not just feeling sick, she began to lose consciousness.

Mistakenly believing her to be falling asleep, Leslie and the rest of the group put their friend to bed. Laying her carefully on her side, they placed a bucket on the floor, in case of emergency. It wasn't too long before the bucket became necessary. However, Veronica rolled over and vomited all over the bed and did not wake up.

Vomiting without waking up is a sign of possible alcohol poisoning. It is a life-threatening situation and is an important warning sign that you should call for medical assistance immediately. When I spoke about this to the group, Leslie and Sian became even more concerned about Veronica than they were before and that is why they decided to talk to me.

They wanted to know how they could approach their friend about this problem without making her feel uncomfortable. Apparently Veronica had a range of other problems to deal with, including some unpleasant family issues, and Leslie felt that if they did not deal with this in a sensitive manner it could result in their friend feeling even more alone than she already did. They did not want to lose their friend—when she was sober she was a great girl—but her drinking behaviour was becoming increasingly dangerous and was putting them all at risk. How could they handle this very complex issue with sensitivity but still get a very important message across to their friend?

Leslie and Sian were very distressed when they spoke to me. They had been extremely worried about their friend's welfare for some time, but now that they realised she could have died, the need to respond in some way became much more urgent.

The most important thing to do in these cases is, first, to make sure that the young person who is raising the issue is supported in some way. It's all well and good to try to provide information to give to the person with the alcohol problem, but often the concerned young person needs just as much support. Often they have been burdened by their concern over their friend's alcohol use for some time. They haven't shared their worries with anybody and it has become a bigger and bigger problem over time.

After they have aired their concerns, reassure them that they were right to do so. Make sure you ask them how they are feeling after they have shared the information—check that they are okay about what they have said and that they do not feel guilty about possibly betraying their friend's trust. Do they feel better now? Are they relieved that they have got it all off their chest? In my experience, the sense of relief that many of these teenagers feel after they have expressed their concerns is unbelievable. Often just sharing the problem with a responsible adult removes a huge burden from a teenager who is concerned about a friend.

Here are just a few examples of some of the issues that young people are coping with. Some of these are extreme cases while others are not at all unusual. For each of these, the young person who shared their story had had to deal with the problem for some time before sharing it with a responsible adult who they felt could assist them in some way. As I'm sure you'll agree, it must have been a tremendous burden for such a young person to shoulder.

Shauna was extremely concerned about one of her friends, Joelle. Joelle was a big drinker and when she became very drunk she would become depressed and would cut herself. This started a few months ago and had recently been getting worse. Shauna wanted to know how to approach her friend and also how to deal with her self-harm issues. What should she do?

Mike and his best mate Brad were both in year eleven. Mike had been worried about his friend's drinking for some time. They had been drinking together for a couple of years but it seemed to Mike that Brad's drinking was getting completely out of control. It was not unusual for Brad to drink at least a bottle of bourbon on a Saturday night, and lately he was drinking just as much on a Friday evening. Some weekends he was even drinking on Sunday afternoon.

What had really freaked Mike out, however, was the discovery that Brad now drank during the week. He had found this out by accident after visiting his friend one evening after school and walking in on him gulping down a glass of bourbon. Brad laughed it off and said that he was having a drink to calm him down after a big day, but his mate became really worried. Isn't that what alcoholics do? The young man did not know where to go next. Who should he talk to and how could he deal with this problem without jeopardising a friendship he really valued?

Ella had been going out with Neil for six months and the relationship was going really well, apart from when he was drunk. Ella lived in a small country town and most of the parties that she attended with Neil were at properties outside town. Before they went they would usually negotiate some basic rules about how they would get home, with the usual decision being that they would stay overnight on the property.

Often, however, this was not what ended up happening. Once Neil had been drinking for a while, his personality changed and he became very aggressive. Even though they had planned to stay at the property, halfway through the night he usually changed his mind and would decide to drive back to town, demanding that Ella go with him.

Ella did not want to get into a car with her drunken boyfriend. She was frightened for his safety as well as her own, but Neil was a scary character when he was drunk and she did not feel that she could argue with him. She had driven back to town with him many times but was becoming more and more concerned about this dangerous behaviour.

When she tried to raise this with Neil when he was sober, however, he had no recollection of his aggressive behaviour. He could not remember how he had got home and refused to discuss the issue with Ella. She wanted some strategies for dealing with a boyfriend who obviously had a drinking problem. The worst thing was that he was not only putting his own life at risk—he was also jeopardising Ella's.

Sometimes it's not just their friends that young people worry about. A relative's alcohol use, particularly a parent's, can be just as concerning for teenagers.

Peta, a year twelve student, believed that her mother was an alcoholic. She did not approach me for advice or information—she simply wanted to share her story because she was concerned that even though I warned about some of the short-term harms associated with alcohol, I failed to mention the possibility of long-term dependence.

Her mother had had a problem with alcohol for as long as she could remember, although she believed that it had got worse since her parents' divorce. Just some of the incidents that she shared with me were as follows: the nights that she had to put her mother to bed after she had become too drunk to make it to the bedroom; the many times that her mother had either driven her to or from school intoxicated; and the evening Peta had to take her mother to the emergency department of the local hospital after a drunken fall had resulted in a broken arm.

Peta was definitely street-smart. She had had to grow up very quickly and, as a result, she had a very mature attitude towards alcohol. She rarely drank, and when she did it was usually only a very small amount. She had seen the 'ugly' side of alcohol and it had had an enormous impact on her life. She wanted more young people to know that this was a very real consequence when alcohol was abused.

It is vital that parents communicate with their children about the role that alcohol plays in their lives. Although there are cases where there are indeed great problems, there are many other times when unnecessary distress could easily be prevented simply by talking.

> Daniel, a year ten student from an inner-city school, spoke to me about someone he knew who drank every evening—a couple of glasses of alcohol—and how worried he was about what this might be doing to the person's health.
>
> By the way Daniel was talking I was convinced he was speaking about one of his peers, another year ten student. Daily drinking by a school-based young person is highly problematic and I began to give some advice to Daniel about how to intervene. But his response to my advice made it clear that the person he was worried about was not a friend. It suddenly dawned on me that he was talking about his father.
>
> When he finally confirmed that it was indeed his father Daniel was talking about, it immediately became a very different story. His father was coming home from work and having a couple of glasses of wine. There was no evidence of excessive alcohol consumption and Daniel admitted that there were many nights when his father drank nothing at all. Did he ever see his dad drunk? I asked him. He shook his head. From the information I was given it sounded as though there was no significant alcohol problem. Daniel appeared to be worried about nothing—the only real problem was that the family never spoke about alcohol and how it was used in their home.

Alcohol is not going to go away. It is such a huge part of what defines us as Australians that it may be quite challenging for many of us to acknowledge that it can cause major problems in people's lives.

Positive conversations with your children about alcohol and the role it plays in your family will help your sons and daughters to develop a healthier attitude towards this popular drug. As a parent it is vital that you discuss that some adults experience problems with their drinking. Too often, the fact that alcohol is a significant community issue is ignored in favour of highlighting the youth alcohol problem. Sharing any useful strategies that you may have developed in helping friends and family members in this area could assist your child to deal with friends they believe are exhibiting similar problems.

• If I call an ambulance because a friend gets into trouble, will the police become involved?

One of the most important messages we must get across to young people is the need to call for medical assistance should someone they know get into trouble. What 'get into trouble' actually means can be interpreted in many ways. If someone loses consciousness and can't be woken up it is clearly a medical emergency, but I usually tell young people that if they're unsure, if something doesn't feel right, it is appropriate to call for help.

One of the major barriers to young people calling for help is the fear that there may be police involvement—that is, if they call an ambulance, the police will automatically become involved. It's always interesting to break this fear down with school students. On first glance it would appear that it has something to do with a fear of the police and that they could get into trouble with the law. When you scratch the surface, though, you quickly discover that it has far more to do with their parents finding out that they have done the 'wrong thing'. I'm not saying that these young people *aren't* worried about getting into trouble with the law—they are! It's just that for many teenagers, getting into trouble with the law usually means that you let your parents down, and most young people don't want that.

When answering whether police would respond to an ambulance call, you have to be very careful because there is no clear-cut response. There are always examples that will challenge what the rules are meant to be.

Sixteen-year-old Tran attended one of my education sessions at his school. During the session I had been asked whether the police became involved if a young person called an ambulance to a person who was drunk or who had taken illegal drugs, and I had told them that this was typically not the case. In the small group session after the presentation, Tran wanted to share his story as he felt that it contradicted the information I had given.

A few weeks before, Tran and a group of friends had gone out for a big night. Instead of going to a party, the group of friends decided to meet in a local park—a regular hangout for young people in his area on a Saturday night. They had all been drinking for some time when it became obvious that one of the boys was in trouble. He had lost consciousness and, no matter what any of them did, they were unable to rouse him. After some discussion they decided to call an ambulance. Within a few minutes it had arrived and the officers had swung into action.

The unconscious boy was taken by the ambulance to the local hospital with one of the group accompanying him. The rest of the boys were left in the park, all feeling a little shell-shocked by what had just happened. Minutes later, a police car pulled up. Two officers approached the group and gave cautions to two of them for possession of alcohol by minors.

Had the police been called to the park by the ambulance officers, and did they just wait until the ambulance had left to pounce on them? Tran wanted to know.

After discussion with a number of police officers around the country about this story and others like it, all I can say is that it's important for us to let our young people know that there are no hard and fast rules when it comes to this issue. Most importantly, though, it is vital that young people are aware that when a call is put out for an ambulance, that is exactly what you get. You will call 000 and be asked by the 000 operator what service you require. If you request an ambulance you will be put through to the ambulance operator, who will ask for the relevant details regarding the incident and location. When the call gets put out, it is put out on the ambulance radio lines, completely different lines to that which police listen to. As a result, the police are unaware that the call even exists.

There are some occasions, however, particularly in regional centres, when an ambulance is not able to get to the incident fast enough (usually because they are dealing with another emergency) and, as a result, the police are sent to the scene. At these times the police are not there to lecture or get people into trouble, they are simply there to ensure that the person in trouble is kept safe until the ambulance arrives.

So what could have happened in the story Tran told above? One explanation I have been given by police is that sometimes, when an ambulance has been called out to a party or to a gathering of young people (such as in a park), a neighbour or some other interested member of the public will call the police to report it. Once the police have been called, they have no choice but to attend the incident. Another possibility could be that the ambulance officers were sufficiently concerned about the remaining young men in the park that they put a call in to police.

So what message should you give your child in response to this question? It needs to be remembered that there are no guarantees here, but essentially it is highly unlikely that the police will attend an ambulance call unless there is another crime committed—for example, a fight breaks out or weapons are observed by ambulance staff. It is important to remember that even if the police do attend, they are not there to harass the person who is unwell, or their friends.

It is up to you as parents to ensure that your children feel confident enough in their relationship with you that they do not fear the possibility of police involvement. I've said it before and I'll say it again: every time your child leaves the house they need to know that they can call you for your help, any time of the day or night, no matter what they have done. This unconditional commitment to your child will help erase any barriers to them asking for help for themselves or their friends.

• Would the hospital call my parents if I was hospitalised after drinking too much?

This is a very similar question to the previous one, but much more difficult to answer. Over the years I've had the question asked in a number of different ways, including:

- If I take a friend to hospital will my parents be called?
- Would I need to give my full name to the hospital if I took a friend to hospital after they have drunk too much?
- Would my parents be charged for my time in hospital?
- Can I give a fake name if I get taken to hospital? What happens to me if I get caught using a false name?

And the list goes on and on. As you can see, they are all versions of the same concern: What if my parents discover that I have been drinking?

I'm sure I should say here that if you have a good and honest relationship with your child and you maintain open lines of communication they will not have these concerns, but in reality there's always going to be a certain degree of shame associated with getting into trouble with the police or being hospitalised after drinking too much or taking other drugs. There are going to be very few young people who feel confident enough in themselves, let alone in their relationship with their parents, to feel okay about being hospitalised after a big night out. If they can avoid being discovered, they're going to feel much better about it.

I've discussed this question with emergency departments across the country, and I have to say that this is an incredibly complex area and there are no simple answers. Hospitals are hesitant to give too many details because there is always a tabloid newspaper or current affairs show ready to attack them either for being irresponsible by not calling parents if their child has been admitted or putting young people at risk by making the call. They really can't win no matter what they do!

The one thing that seems fairly clear is that if the young person is under sixteen years of age, the hospital has no choice. In those cases, they must contact the parent. When it comes to those aged sixteen or seventeen, however, the rules appear to be a little more fluid. Hospital staff stress that decisions are made on a case-by-case basis, and in my experience the response is very much dependent on the staff who are on duty at the time. One of the emergency department workers I spoke to told me a story that highlights why different staff may respond in a particular way when a young person is brought in after drinking too much.

Narelle, the mother of two teenage sons, was a senior nurse in the emergency department of a busy inner-city hospital. One Saturday night a young man was wheeled into the department by ambulance officers. He was having difficulty breathing and was on a respirator. A friend was accompanying him, and he also appeared to be quite intoxicated.

The young man had lost control of his bodily functions. As well as being drenched in vomit, he had wet himself and it smelt as if he had emptied his bowels. He was a total mess and was obviously going to be with the staff for some time.

Details were taken from the friend and, after finding out that the patient was sixteen years old, staff had to decide whether to call his parents or not. It was then that Narelle noticed the T-shirt that the boy was wearing. She had bought exactly the same one for her eldest son for his birthday. It was then that she made the decision to call the parents. This boy could have been her son and, if it was her, she would have wanted to be there with him.

Although there were such varied responses from hospital staff I spoke to as to their procedures and protocols in this area, one thing remained constant—they wanted young people to feel that they could call an ambulance without fear.

Regardless of whether parents are called or not, we need to ensure that our children continue to seek medical assistance should something go wrong. The only way this is going to happen is if we make it really easy for them to do so by making sure that any barrier to them making the call to an ambulance is reduced whenever possible.

When you have a conversation around calling an ambulance and hospitalisation, let your child know that if they are going to call for help they have your complete support in doing so. You hope that they will never have to do it but, if they do, tell them that after they have made the call to the ambulance, you expect them to make a second call to you to inform them about the emergency. You want to be there with them, to support them through this scary time. It's a big thing to call 000—adults find it confronting, it must be terrifying for a teenager!

4
CANNABIS

Marijuana, pot, dope, weed, grass, spin, ganga, hash, mull . . . these are just some of the street terms that Australians use for cannabis. The wide variety of names reflects the drug's popularity among certain groups of people in the community.

Cannabis continues to be the most popular illegal drug in Australia and around the world. For many years when I visited schools cannabis was the substance that most of the teaching staff wanted me to talk to their students about. Through the 1980s and 90s, cannabis use across the community continued to increase, with particular concern focused on the increasing number of school-based young people who were experimenting with the drug.

Although we now see almost as many young females as males experimenting with cannabis, girls do not use as much of the drug, or use it as often, as their male peers. As a result, young men are far more likely to have problems with their cannabis use.

Cannabis was also the drug that I was asked the most questions about in the school setting, sometimes even exceeding the number asked about alcohol. As we see more and more with alcohol nowadays, young cannabis users developed a whole mythology around their drug of choice, often in an attempt to justify their drug use. This was particularly true in their perception of cannabis as a 'herb' or being 'natural', which somehow meant that the harms associated with its use were perceived as being not as great and, in some cases, even non-existent.

Since that time, cannabis use among school-based young people in Australia has halved. That said, it still continues to be the illicit drug most commonly used by school students.

This decrease in use appears to be consistent with an incredible change in attitude towards cannabis by young people. No longer is it regarded as the 'cool' thing to do, with many young people now seeing it as a 'loser's drug'. As one young woman explained to me when I asked her to describe the cannabis users in her year twelve class, 'They're the guys who can't get dates, sit at home on the weekend watching DVDs and eating pizza!'

Even though its popularity is waning, it still continues to be the illicit drug that many parents fear, mainly because in most cases of young people experimenting with illegal substances, cannabis will be the first that they try. As a result, it is also often the first that parents find out about—and when they *do* find out, they have a multitude of questions and assumptions based on misinformation and fear, for example:

- Will this be the start of a slippery slope into other drug use, ending with heroin?
- Cannabis is not the same as it used to be; it's 'super strength' now. What will that do to my child's brain?
- It'll cause my child to lose motivation, drop out of school and have no future.
- They've broken one law; next they'll become dealers and members of international crime gangs.

Now the last one may be a little extreme, but I'm sure you get the picture! Let me make one thing perfectly clear—I'm not saying that any parent who discovers their child is experimenting with any illegal drug, including cannabis, has no cause for concern. Far from it; at the very least your child is breaking the law and the implications of that can be immense. There is also a range of possible physical, psychological and social consequences associated with any drug use that need to be considered. Before you go off the deep end, however, it is important to look at the situation rationally and with the benefit of good-quality, accurate information.

Without a doubt, most young Australians will come into contact with cannabis at some time in their lives. Most of them will make the decision not to use the drug, but others will be inquisitive and wonder what all the fuss is about. As a result they will experiment and, unfortunately, some of them will experience great problems as a consequence.

Experts estimate that about one in ten people who use cannabis will go on to experience some sort of problem with the drug. That's not particularly good odds. These problems can be significant and affect every aspect of their life.

For the other 90 per cent, their experiments with cannabis will, for the most part, be problem-free. Therein lies our greatest obstacle in providing accurate information about cannabis. The majority of users actually experience very few problems and our young people are well aware of this. They can identify classmates who are users or know of older siblings who smoke and don't appear to have major issues as a result of their use. If we try to tell them otherwise, they are likely to reject the messages we are giving them and we will lose our credibility. Of course, most parents lose their credibility in the area of alcohol and other drugs pretty quickly! It only takes one careless comment or using the wrong street name for a particular drug and you will be regarded as 'old' and 'past it'. However, there is a way of regaining some credibility, particularly around cannabis, and that is by giving your teenagers some information on the drug that challenges them and gets them to think critically about what they have heard from friends.

Debunking myths that young people believe to be true is the best way to win them over. I do it every day when I give talks in schools. I highlight a myth that is currently doing the rounds and then give them the real story. In this chapter you will find a number of cannabis-related questions, some of which are based on such myths. Try to use some of these in conversations to maintain or win back some credibility.

First, though, I'll give you a piece of advice that I received from one of my bosses many years ago in regard to drug information. I continue to live by it to this day.

I was just starting out in the field of alcohol and other drugs and was attending many seminars and information sessions. With every talk I went to I became more confused, as each piece of information seemed to contradict the last one I had heard. I couldn't work out what I was meant to believe and what was factually inaccurate.

When I told my boss about my dilemma he said, 'Just remember that there are no definites when it comes to drugs. There are lots of "possibles", "probables" and "maybes", but no "definites". If you are ever in a presentation and someone starts telling you that a drug is going to do this to you, or that to you, calmly put your pen down, close your notebook and leave the lecture immediately. That person doesn't know what they're talking about.'

If you always remember that there are no 'definites' when it comes to drugs, that there are no right or wrong answers, it will make your life much easier, particularly when talking to your children. Conversations about the issue will be less confrontational and more balanced. Just remember that everyone is different and every person who uses a drug will have a different experience to some degree.

When you decide to have a conversation with your child about any illicit drug, including cannabis, remember that there are no black and white answers, only shades of grey. Some people will progress to using other drugs, some won't. Cannabis use will lead to mental health problems for some young people, others won't have any problems at all. Although some parents are hesitant to use this approach, believing that the resulting message is not strong enough, the truth is that not always knowing what will happen is just as scary and just as powerful. It is also much more effective than lying to your child in an attempt to frighten them off drug use.

When you acknowledge individual differences and let your teenager know that there are no guarantees when it comes to the use of any drug, you are being honest with your child, and in doing so showing them that you want to maintain open and frank communication with them in the future. Grounded in that type of approach, hopefully some of the information presented in this chapter will help you to have positive and productive conversations around cannabis.

• If my child has used cannabis, does this mean they will go on to use harder drugs?

Carol was the mother of three girls, the eldest of whom, Courtney, was at university. Courtney had always tried to 'push boundaries'. She had been a big drinker during her high school years but in recent years had appeared to calm down a bit. Carol was worried about the effect that Courtney's behaviour would have on her younger daughters, so she had come down hard on her drinking and warned her that she would never tolerate illicit drug use.

I met Carol when I was visiting a school community. She approached me to ask for my advice as she had recently found a bag of what she believed to be cannabis in her daughter's room. She was terribly distressed. Not only did she now believe Courtney was a drug user, she also felt deeply betrayed. Carol had told her that this behaviour was simply not acceptable and Courtney seemed to have ignored this. There was also a great deal of fear.

'Where does she go from here?' Carol asked me. 'If she's using this now, what will she be experimenting with in the future?'

Over the years I have spoken to many parents who have found themselves in exactly the same situation as Carol. No matter how much you may prepare yourself for the day that you discover your child has used an illegal drug, the impact is still devastating. So many thoughts are likely to go through your head but inevitably the fear of progression to other drugs is one of the greatest fears that parents have.

One of the most popular myths about drugs is the belief that if you start using cannabis it will lead to heroin use. This is known as the 'gateway theory', and is frequently used in an attempt to scare young people off experimenting with a range of drugs, but most particularly cannabis.

This theory comes from studies of heroin users which show that they have almost all used cannabis at some time or another. However, it definitely doesn't mean that all cannabis users will eventually use heroin. In fact, over a third of the Australian population have tried cannabis at one time, whereas only a very small percentage (2 per cent) have ever tried heroin. If the gateway theory is true, there should be far more heroin users in this country.

Undoubtedly, experimenting with cannabis puts you at risk of coming into contact with a range of other drugs. A person who is selling you cannabis may have other drugs on offer and this easy access to illegal substances could result in a young person being more likely to experiment. There is also the possibility that after breaking one taboo—smoking an illegal drug like cannabis—it is much easier to break another. In my experience, though, most teenagers have 'drawn their own line in the sand' (as most adults do) and have established which drugs they're going to try and which they're not. For many it would appear that these choices are made early in adolescence. Once they've made that decision you could throw drugs at them and they still wouldn't try them.

So is there a gateway drug?

It is now believed that the environment that a young person is exposed to has a much stronger influence on what drug is used in the future, rather than there being a logical progression from one drug to another. That is, if it's easier for a young person to get their hands on cannabis than alcohol, then it's more likely they will smoke pot. This is known as the 'common liability model'. It states the likelihood that the movement of use from one drug to another is not necessarily determined by the previous use of a particular drug, but instead by the young person's individual tendencies and environmental circumstances.

Interestingly, research has shown that regular heavy alcohol use, particularly during the early teens, is possibly the strongest predictor of future illicit drug use. Of course, this does not fit into the messages that most parents want to give their children about drug use—alcohol is a legal drug, one which the vast majority of Australians use on a regular basis. However, excessive drinking by young people causes many problems and particular patterns of use are regarded as possible indicators of future illicit drug use.

• Is cannabis really 30 times stronger than it used to be?

In recent years, stories have done the rounds describing a 'super-strength' cannabis that is up to 30 times more potent than it was a decade ago. This story is often used to emphasise the potential dangers of the drug and why we should be even more concerned about our children experimenting with it now than in the past.

It's also an argument used by parents who experimented with cannabis during their youth to justify their own drug use and at the same time warn their children against trying the drug.

Beth, 42, has three teenage boys. Although she has no hard proof, she is pretty sure that at least one of her sons has experimented with cannabis. Beth was a teenager in the 70s and did occasionally have a puff on a joint during her university years. She never really enjoyed the experience but would have a smoke once in a while because it was there.

Summoning up the courage to discuss the issue of drugs with her children, Beth used a quiet time in the car to raise the topic. When she asked her eldest son whether he had ever used cannabis, he fired the question right back at her: 'Have you ever smoked dope, Mum?'

'Well, it was a long time ago and yes, I did have a few puffs when I was at uni, but it's a different story now. Cannabis is a very different drug. It's much stronger now than it was then and much more dangerous.'

What a cop-out! Beth did use the drug, but she tried to get out of it by claiming that the drug she used was somehow less harmful than the one her son may potentially use. Cannabis is cannabis is cannabis. Even if it is stronger, which we will discuss in a moment, does that really make much of a difference? On pages 175–183 we'll look at how a parent should deal with answering questions about their previous drug use, but for now let's just look at the evidence for the response Beth gave.

First off, let's think about this for a couple of seconds. If we could really make a plant 30 or so times stronger than it was ten years ago, why haven't we done that to other plants and crops? If we had the technology and know-how we could now have strawberries the size of watermelons and we could have gone a long way towards solving the world's food-shortage problem! Although selective crossbreeding programs have increased the potency of cannabis to some degree, it would be impossible to increase it by this much. Genetically engineering a plant to make it substantially stronger over such a short period of time is just plain science fiction. So why do people believe that cannabis is so much stronger than it used to be? Even long-term cannabis users will tell you that their drug of choice is much more potent now than when they first started using it.

To answer this question, let's consider what we measure when we examine strength or 'potency'.

Cannabis comes from the *Cannabis sativa* plant. It contains more than 400 chemicals, 60 of which fit into a category called cannabinoids. The main ingredient in cannabis that is responsible for the psychoactive, or mood-altering, effects is called delta-9-tetrahydrocannabinol, or 'THC' for short. As the level of THC is not always the same from plant to plant, we measure the amount of THC found in the individual plant, or part of the plant, to determine its strength or potency.

The THC content of a plant can depend on a number of things, including the way in which the plant is grown, the part of the plant that is used and the way the plant is prepared for use.

Normally, the male cannabis plant fertilises the female plant. If female plants are grown in isolation, then the flowering tops of the plant remain unfertilised. These unfertilised flowering tops, known as sinsemilla, have particularly high THC levels. Crossbreeding of plants can also produce strains of the cannabis plant that have particularly high levels of THC.

Some argue that cannabis grown hydroponically, which refers to the method of growing plants under artificial light, is stronger than cannabis grown outdoors or in natural light conditions (this cannabis is often known as 'bush buds' or 'bush weed'). Users of the drug say they can tell when they are using 'hydro' cannabis versus bush buds because the effects are so much stronger. However, research conducted around the world has shown that this is not necessarily the case.

One of the most important things to remember is that certain parts of the plant have much higher concentrations of THC, such as the flowering tops, 'heads' or 'buds'. The leaves contain lower levels, with very little THC being found in the stalks and seeds of the cannabis plant. What we do know is that there is now much greater availability of the heads or buds than there was in the past. This means that cannabis users of today have greater access to stronger THC products. Years ago, the only part of the plant that was widely available was leaf, which has comparatively low levels of THC. Now that people are more likely to smoke flowering heads, it makes sense that they are experiencing more of an effect and thus believe that the drug is more potent than ever before. However, this does not mean that the plant itself has become significantly stronger.

In the US, THC levels of cannabis have risen slightly over the last 25 years, from about 1 per cent to 4 per cent. In New Zealand, the potency of THC has not changed. In Europe, cannabis has remained the same in most places, except the Netherlands, where an increase in potency has occurred, mainly due to the cannabis industry that exists in that country.

To sum up, the strength of cannabis does seem to have increased over the last 25 years, but it is very unlikely that it has become 30 times stronger. But even if potency had increased in the recent past, it would not necessarily mean that smoking the drug had become more dangerous. In fact, the major health risk associated with cannabis comes from the fact that it is *smoked*. As a result, cannabis smokers experience all of the same problems as tobacco smokers.

The question of potency often confuses the whole cannabis issue. Whatever its potency, cannabis is not harmless. We need to make sure that our young people are well informed about the risks associated with the drug, and not get so hung up on whether or not the drug has become stronger.

• Cannabis is natural. Doesn't that mean it is safer than man-made drugs?

If I had a dollar for every time I've heard this come out of a sixteen-year-old boy's mouth, I'd be a very rich man! It's a comment that continues to astound me though, for the whole concept of something being safe just because it's 'natural' is really quite ludicrous.

Natural does not mean safe. Natural substances can be just as harmful, and in some cases even more harmful, than synthetically made substances. Mother Nature has done an extremely good job of producing a whole range of substances, including many drugs, which are far more powerful and much more dangerous than man-made drugs.

I don't know what happens to young men around the age of fifteen or sixteen. All of a sudden, for no apparent reason, a small group of them decide that things which grow in the ground are 'natural' and 'herbs' and that they should start smoking them!

Cannabis has long been the favourite of those looking for 'natural highs' and, even though use of the drug among young people continues to drop, some teenagers continue to experiment by puffing on a bong or lighting up a joint. Although the statistics don't support it, I also believe that there are a growing number of young people who experiment with other naturally occurring hallucinogens, such as magic mushrooms.

In recent years we have tried hard to get the message across to teenagers about the dangers associated with drugs like ecstasy and amphetamines. Part of that message has been that they are manufactured in backyard laboratories using a variety of dangerous chemicals. What we have not done is evaluate this message very carefully. Are there other messages that young people are picking up inadvertently as a result of highlighting the dangers of 'chemical-based products'? It appears that some adolescents now regard naturally occurring substances like cannabis and psilocybin (found in magic mushrooms) as 'healthy' alternatives.

The word 'natural' is often used in advertising and marketing to imply that a product is healthy. In reality, 'natural' doesn't mean very much at all, particularly in terms of safety. In fact, there may even be some benefits in using a drug that is man-made, the most important being that if it comes from a reputable source, you know exactly what is contained in it. Pharmaceutical drugs go through a rigorous manufacturing process and all of the ingredients are checked and rechecked. You know what dose you are taking and this helps to reduce possible negative consequences. Now that doesn't mean that things can't go wrong with pharmaceutical drugs—far from it! But there is quality control. When it comes to a drug like cannabis, however, there is no way of knowing what dosage you are using. There is no simple test to identify the THC content of the plant and it can therefore be very difficult to determine how much to use, other than trial and error—that is, smoke a little and see what happens! Unfortunately, for some people the result can be frightening.

Using any drug, whether it be natural or not, entails some degree of risk. This is particularly true if you are naïve about the effects, as this story illustrates.

> While working in a medical tent at an underage dance party we were visited by a group of young girls who were extremely distressed. They were carrying one of their friends who appeared to be fitting. Carrie looked extremely unwell and we were unable to rouse her to get any information. Her friends assured us that she had not taken drugs or alcohol. There was certainly no smell of alcohol on her breath and according to her friends she had no medical condition that could have caused the problem.
>
> Just as we were preparing to transport her to hospital she came to, apparently no worse for wear. Away from her friends we asked her what had happened. Slightly embarrassed, she told us that she had gone to the toilet and had met up with a group of girls from her old school. She had been offered a joint by one of the girls and had reluctantly accepted. She went into the toilet cubicle and had taken a few drags of the joint and then hurried back to her friends. That was all that she remembered.

This is an extreme example but highlights one of the risks of cannabis use. Like any drug, cannabis is unpredictable: even if you have used it many times, there is always the possibility that something could go wrong.

Another issue to consider when talking about natural products is that when it comes to substances that can be found in plant matter, such as magic mushrooms, many trees and plants look very similar. The wrong plant could be chosen and something highly poisonous could be ingested. Over the years there have been cases of young people selecting the wrong mushroom or piece of bark and finding themselves in hospital or dead due to poisoning.

A drug is a drug, and whether it's natural or man-made there are harms associated with its use. It doesn't matter whether you get it from a doctor, the local bottle shop or a dealer, it is not risk-free. And those risks are going to be different for every person using the drug, each time they use it.

• Isn't cannabis legal in some parts of Australia?

Cannabis is illegal in every state and territory across Australia. Because the laws are different across the country there seems to be a great deal of confusion surrounding the legal status of cannabis. The belief that the drug is legal in some jurisdictions, usually South Australia and the Australian Capital Territory, is probably due to the fact that they were the first two places to decriminalise cannabis (the former in 1987 and the latter in 1993). The changes to the laws in these places attracted a lot of attention at the time and some people are still not sure what the story is.

I can't tell you how many times I've been told by young men living in New South Wales that they can't wait until they get their driver's licence so they can go to Canberra and 'bong on' in the mall. Boy would they be in for a big surprise if they tried to do that!

Decriminalising cannabis does not mean that the drug is now legal, like alcohol and tobacco. The law has changed in some places so that minor cannabis offences, such as the possession of a small amount of the drug for personal use, can be dealt with through a 'civil penalty' rather than a criminal charge. In the case of cannabis, the civil penalty is usually a fine, similar to what you would pay if you were caught speeding.

In other parts of the country any cannabis offence is a criminal offence. If someone is charged with possession of cannabis in these areas and found guilty, they could receive a large fine and a criminal record. In some cases they might find themselves in jail.

To make the matter even more confusing, some states have a 'cautioning' program. Each program is different, but if a police officer finds someone using cannabis they have the power to administer a 'caution' instead of putting them into the court system. This may involve the person having to attend an information session or be assessed by a health professional for possible cannabis-related problems. Although all programs are different, information on the cannabis user is collected and only a certain number of cautions are allowed before further legal ramifications come into play.

Some people are not too happy about the changes in the laws around cannabis. Some say it 'sends the wrong message' and is 'going soft' on cannabis users. However, one of the main reasons the laws were changed was because it was usually adolescents that were getting into trouble with cannabis. They would experiment with the drug, get caught, and then find themselves with a criminal record for the rest of their lives. Sometimes this had life-changing repercussions.

Many years ago I was working with a sporting organisation that regularly sent team members overseas on training camps and exchange programs. One day I received a phone call from a young athlete who had just been refused entry into the US due to a prior drug conviction.

The young man was terribly confused. He had no idea what they were referring to and had called me for advice. It finally came out that he had indeed received a criminal conviction for cannabis use when he was fifteen years old. He had been caught smoking cannabis in a park with some of his mates and his parents had been called. A dumb decision made several years before had altered this young man's life forever. He was unable to go to the planned training camp in the US and dropped out of the sport a short time later.

For many young people, getting caught using cannabis and being given a caution is enough of a punishment to deter them from ever using again. There are others, however, who are not going to stop whatever we do.

As a parent it is extremely important that you discuss the legal consequences of drug use with your child. As much as we talk about the physical and mental health effects of drug use, it is usually the social impacts, such as the legal ramifications, that are going to affect the majority of our teenagers. Getting caught with an illegal drug can change their life forever.

They also need to be aware that hanging out with friends who smoke cannabis can also get you into trouble. Cannabis has a very strong, distinctive smell. If you sit in a room where it is being smoked, by the end of the night your clothes will probably smell of the drug. Due to a range of law enforcement strategies that are now in place across the country this can have huge implications.

Jake had drawn the short straw and was 'designated driver' for the night. He and his friends were planning to attend a number of parties and because he was on his P plates Jake was well aware that he could not drink at all.

At the first party a number of people were smoking a bong, including two of Jake's friends. When the time came to head off to the next party, his friends piled into the back of his car and Jake drove off. A few kilometres down the road he was pulled over by a random breath testing (RBT) van and asked to submit to a test. Knowing that he had had nothing to drink, Jake agreed to the test. While the police officer was waiting for the result, Jake noticed that he sniffed inside the car. The smell of cannabis was obvious but no one had the drug in their possession so the young man was not particularly worried.

Although the RBT result was negative the police officer asked Jake to step out of the car and submit to a sobriety test. Due to the smell of cannabis, the officer had reason to believe that he might be intoxicated. Jake passed the test with flying colours—so he should have, he was sober—but the officer was not convinced. Jake's friends were obviously drug-affected and the smell of cannabis was on his clothes. He was told that he would need to accompany the officer to the local hospital and submit to a blood test.

Still Jake was not worried. He had not had a drink and he hadn't smoked.

Yet when the results of Jake's blood test came back they were positive. Jake had not smoked cannabis that night and he was not intoxicated when he was driving. But he had smoked in the previous week and because cannabis stays in the system for much longer than other drugs, he had returned a positive test. His charge of driving while under the influence of an illegal drug could change his life.

Young people also need to understand that police now have sniffer dogs. Even if they don't have drugs on them, if someone has been around cannabis or people who smoke the drug they might be searched. Although the laws are slightly different in each state and territory, police are authorised to use drug sniffer dogs to search people at random in three situations: in pubs and other places where alcohol is served; at entertainment events, including sporting events, concerts, dance parties and street parades; and on public transport and in stations. If a dog sits down next to someone, police can search that person.

When you talk to your child about the law, it is important that you discuss the issue of sniffer dogs. These animals are not infallible—they often sit down in front of people who have no drugs on them—so all young people need to be told what to do in these circumstances.

Most importantly, they should stay calm and be polite. They could be fined or arrested if they don't cooperate with the police. They should let the police search them but they have the right to ask why they are being searched and should ask the officer for their name, rank and station.

Bonita was nineteen years old and was attending her first big dance party when a group of police and sniffer dogs arrived. When she walked through the gates into the event she found a dog sitting in front of her, and a plainclothes police woman asked her whether she was carrying drugs.

'It all happened so fast,' she told me later. 'I didn't even know that there were any dogs at the party until one was in front of me. The police woman was really nice and asked me a lot of questions, most of which I don't remember now. I've never taken drugs and I certainly didn't have any on me when I went into the party.

'All I remember is emptying my pockets, taking my shoes and socks off, and telling the lady that I didn't do drugs. I don't think she believed me. The worst thing was seeing all these people watching as I was being frisked by the officer and knowing that I had done nothing wrong!'

Once the officer was satisfied that Bonita did not have any drugs on her she was free to go. Although she did not use drugs herself, Bonita had just been to a party where some people had been smoking dope. It is likely that the dogs detected the cannabis smoke on her clothes and that is what had led to her being searched.

'Guilt by association' is a concept that all young people need to be aware of. No one is asking teenagers to tell their friends what and what not to do. If they do not want to risk the legal consequences of cannabis use, however, protecting oneself is as simple as standing up and casually walking into another room when someone lights up a bong.

Put simply, if you get caught using, possessing, growing or selling cannabis anywhere in Australia, you will be punished in some way. This could involve a caution, a fine or some form of intervention, including jail time. It is also important to remember that the more times you get caught, the greater the punishment.

• Does cannabis really cause mental health problems?

Sean was sixteen years old when I met him. He had started using cannabis when he was thirteen, and had smoked regularly since that time. His parents had built him a granny flat above the garage and he would invite his friends over most weekends to share a few bongs. He had never had a bad experience and thought that he was one of those lucky people who could use the drug with few problems. But that proved not to be the case . . .

Three months before I met Sean he had invited his friends over as he had done many times before. The gang were going to watch a DVD, play some video games and eat takeaway. He packed the bong, lit it up and passed it around. When the bong came around the second time something happened to Sean. In his own words, 'his mind snapped'. He could hear voices, very clear voices, that told him in no uncertain terms to kill one of his friends. He shared what was happening to him with one of the other boys in the group, who told him that he was just being 'paranoid'.

Others thought Sean was mucking around when he leapt onto one of his mates. They stopped laughing when they saw blood. Sean had found a small penknife and had stabbed the other boy in the side. As they were all stoned, none of the others present responded quickly, but when they realised just how critical the situation had become they tried to pull Sean off the injured boy. Even though there were five of them, they found it extremely difficult to restrain Sean, and it wasn't until one of them had alerted Sean's parents that they managed to pull him off and start to calm him down.

Sean was hospitalised, put into an adult mental health unit, and given a range of anti-psychotic medication. He had experienced a psychotic episode and was later to discover that he had developed schizophrenia. As a result, Sean would need to be on medication for the rest of his life in order to control the condition.

Cannabis did not cause Sean to develop schizophrenia. He had a family history of schizophrenia (although he did not know it at the time) and using cannabis had 'unlocked' the illness. He may have developed the condition later in life anyway, or he may not have. Regardless, using the drug had brought it on early and had changed his life forever.

He was very keen for me to share his story with other young people. He had been told that cannabis could act as a 'key' to unlock mental health problems such as schizophrenia. But because he had been using the drug for so long and had experienced no problems he thought it was not going to happen to him. He was wrong and he wanted others to learn from his mistake.

The link between cannabis and mental health problems is one that has attracted more attention than any other health effect associated with the drug. Sean's story, although extreme, is all too often a reality for those people who have a pre-existing mental health problem.

The major issue that we face in getting the message across to young people about the risk of mental health problems is that it does not happen to everyone. In fact, most people who smoke cannabis won't experience these types of problems. Teenagers are all too well aware of this and, if we try to tell them otherwise, they are likely to reject all of the messages we give them. We need to be very careful about the information we provide, ensuring that it matches their own experience and has credibility.

Trying to tell a sixteen-year-old that if he smokes pot he'll 'go mad' is likely to be ineffective. Most young people of that age know someone who has smoked cannabis without major side effects, so the message is seen as false.

If that's the case, why do we keep trying to sell this type of message? The main reason is that it's easy; it's black and white and is not too complex. It's also frightening and, once again, we fall back on the old concept of shock tactics—let's provide them with the worst possible scenario and that will stop them from taking part in the activity. Unfortunately, the reality is not that simple and the whole issue of drugs and mental health is full of shades of grey. That's what scares so many parents—when the message gets too difficult there is always the possibility that your child could ask you a question you don't know the answer to and that is terrifying!

Let's try to shed some light on the subject. When we talk about mental health problems and cannabis, we are usually talking about schizophrenia, but in recent times there has also been much more discussion about whether the use of cannabis can lead to other problems, such as depression and anxiety. There has been lots of research to show that there is an 'association' between cannabis use and mental health problems, but this does not necessarily mean that one causes the other.

Some people experience very unpleasant psychological effects when they use cannabis. This usually takes the form of anxiety or panic attacks. In some cases, generally when someone has smoked a lot of the drug, they experience confusion, delusions and, in extreme cases, hallucinations. Although it is rare, some people may experience a short-term psychotic episode (a split from reality) after a heavy session of cannabis use. This can last from several hours up to two or three days. These symptoms are more likely to be felt by people who aren't used to the effects or have smoked more than they are used to. Thankfully, these symptoms are usually short-lived and, as a consequence of the unpleasant experience, many of these people only try it once or twice then never use again.

There are some people, though, who appear to be much more vulnerable to the psychological effects of cannabis. That is, they have a predisposition or a family history of mental illness. For these people, cannabis can 'trigger' a psychotic episode (which they may recover from) or possibly 'unlock' an illness (such as schizophrenia) that may affect them permanently. Younger people appear to be at greater risk of experiencing these effects. As I always say to young people, if you know that you have a family history of mental health problems, it's as if God or fate has written you a big note in red letters saying *Don't use cannabis.*

The link between cannabis and conditions such as depression and anxiety is not clear because, strangely enough, many cannabis users actually smoke the drug in the belief that it will relieve symptoms of these problems. Cannabis may seem to help ease depression when the person is stoned, but once the effects of the drug have worn off, it would appear that it makes depression worse.

The frightening thing for parents who discover that their child is experimenting with cannabis is that, generally speaking, those who start smoking cannabis earlier (in early adolescence) are more likely to experience negative consequences. If they smoke a lot, regularly, then the risks are increased.

When it comes to providing young people with messages about their mental health in relation to cannabis, parents are in a much better position than in the past. Young people today are very tuned into mental health issues and are well aware of conditions such as depression, anxiety and psychosis.

Possibly the most important information you can provide your children with is the mental health history of your family. Do you have family members who have any mental health issues and, if so, which conditions are they? This sort of discussion would never have occurred in the past. There was so much stigma associated with mental health problems that if there was a relative who wasn't well, no one would talk about it either within or outside the family. This stigma has not disappeared, with many Australians still fearing being laughed at or ostracised because of a mental health problem. But you owe it to your children to discuss the issue and, if there is a family history, your children must be told so that they are able to make an informed choice in the future.

If you are finding it difficult to raise the issue of mental health and cannabis, try talking about paranoia. Almost every child, regardless of whether they have had contact with cannabis or not, is aware that this is a side effect of using the drug. Although it may seem quite harmless and almost funny in some contexts ('Are you talking about me?'), paranoia can actually be an early warning sign for friends of cannabis users, particularly if it starts slipping into the person's everyday life, even when they're not stoned.

Once again, most teenagers want strategies to look after themselves and their friends. Asking them to be on the lookout for signs of possible mental health problems in their friends who use cannabis could be useful to them and a great conversation starter.

• Are bongs safer than joints? What about eating cannabis?

At the peak time of cannabis interest, I was regularly asked about the 'safety' of bongs in my visits to schools. It never ceases to amaze me how many young people believe that a bong is actually a safer way to smoke cannabis than a joint.

For the uninitiated, a bong (also known as a water pipe), is a smoking device generally used to smoke cannabis, tobacco or a variety of other substances. A bong is different from smoking a pipe or cigarette in two major ways—first, the water at the bottom of the container cools the smoke before it enters the user's lungs (making it easier to inhale), and second, it allows a much larger amount of smoke to be inhaled quickly as opposed to smaller, more frequent inhalations of pipe and cigarette smoking.

To use a bong, the base of the pipe is usually filled with water. Other liquids, including alcohol, can be used but water is preferred. The cannabis is packed into a 'cone' on the side of the bong and then lit. The user puts their mouth over the mouthpiece or opening and inhales. This causes the flame to be drawn towards the cannabis. When the user inhales, cannabis smoke is produced and this travels through the pipe to the water. The smoke rises through the water and is cooled. The smoke is then trapped in the air chamber above the water, and the user inhales the cooler smoke.

The main reason that many teenagers believe bongs to be safer is because of the water. Friends have told them that this process actually removes the tar and other carcinogenic material from the smoke, thus reducing some of the risks associated with smoking. They see the proof of this—they think—in the colour of the 'bong water', which is often brown and dirty. But although full of smoke impurities, the water removes little, if any, tar and other harmful material.

Even though smoking through a bong may be better for you than smoking unfiltered smoke, it is definitely not risk-free. In fact, some studies have found that bongs actually filter out more THC (the component that gets you stoned) than they do other tars, thereby requiring users to smoke more to get the same effect.

Bongs—usually made of glass—may be bought from shops around the country, although some jurisdictions are in the process of changing the laws to make it illegal to do so. But many young cannabis users make their own bongs from plastic bottles, traditionally orange juice containers, or aluminum soft-drink cans (these are referred to as 'dry bongs'). It is important to note that homemade bongs can be more dangerous because the plastic or aluminium can give off toxic fumes when heated.

As more and more people are becoming aware of the problems linked with smoking any substance, new equipment or paraphernalia is being manufactured to reduce the harms. For example, vaporisers are devices which heat cannabis to below burning point, but high enough to vaporise the oils within the THC. They allow users to inhale a clear vapour which is less dangerous in terms of smoking problems. Much of the work on vaporisers is a result of the research into the medical use of cannabis.

Sometimes young people think that if they can find another way of using the drug other than smoking it, they will avoid the chances of anything going wrong.

On a holiday to Amsterdam, Esther decided to visit a cannabis cafe. Although the drug is not legal in the Netherlands, its use is tolerated in licensed coffee shops. Esther had never used cannabis before but she had always planned to experiment with the drug when she visited the city. Being a non-smoker, she decided that the safest way to use the drug would be to eat it.

When she got to the cafe she bought a chocolate cookie laced with cannabis. She was wise enough to know that she should be extremely careful about how much she ate at one time, so she ate about a quarter of the cookie and then started reading a magazine. After about half an hour she still didn't feel any different and started to think that maybe she hadn't eaten enough.

She had another quarter and then began to feel very hungry. Before long she had eaten the whole thing! She still didn't feel as though she was actually 'stoned', so she left the cafe and decided to take a walk along one of the city's famous canals.

It wasn't too long before Esther regretted her decision. While she was walking the effects of the entire cookie hit her all at once. She discovered that when cannabis is eaten it takes much longer for the drug to hit and the effect can be very different than when smoked. Esther was experiencing some pretty major hallucinogenic effects and was finding it very difficult to work out what was real and what wasn't. She was also feeling very sick and ended up having to sit down on a bench next to a canal.

Luckily for Esther a police officer found her and, after discovering what had happened, took her back to her hotel. The 'cookie incident', as it is now referred to by Esther and her friends, cost her almost two days of her holiday and taught her a valuable lesson.

Eating cannabis definitely avoids the harmful effects associated with smoking the drug, but it also comes with its own set of problems. It is difficult to work out how much the drug is affecting you and it can have a much more intense effect (usually more hallucinogenic) for a much longer time.

There is no safe way of using cannabis. If you are going to smoke the drug it is important to remember that, whatever the substance, smoking is a very dangerous route of administration. At the very least, using a bong forces the cannabis smoke deeper into the lungs. This exposes more of the lungs to tar and other harmful toxins without necessarily increasing the perceived positive effects, i.e. getting you more stoned. Contrary to what many people believe, a person does not necessarily get more of an effect from a bong.

• When I've started to talk to my child about cannabis he has pointed out that it can be used as a medicine. What do I say to that?

Whenever the subject of cannabis-related harms arises within a group of reasonably intelligent young people it is almost inevitable that the medical use of cannabis comes up. A great way of challenging the problems associated with the use of the drug is to point to the fact that cannabis can't be all that bad if it is used to treat some medical conditions. In fact, this whole argument almost runs hand in hand with the 'it's a herb', 'it's natural' line of reasoning and there are some kids (and many adults too) who love it because it helps to justify their own drug use.

There's no getting away from the fact that the medical uses of cannabis have been recognised for thousands of years. Physicians in ancient China used it to relieve constipation, loss of appetite and pain during childbirth. Many other cultures throughout history have used the plant for a range of therapeutic purposes. However, with the development of pharmaceutical drugs in the twentieth century, herbal cures in general fell into disuse. In recent times, however, more and more people have been searching for alternative remedies that may have fewer side effects than the medicines they have been prescribed by their doctors. Although there are often existing therapies available for the medical conditions cannabis may be used to treat, some people experience severe reactions when they are used, or they simply don't work effectively for them. Cannabis appears to offer an alternative for those people. Some of these conditions include:

- pain relief
- nausea and vomiting, particularly in those people who are having chemotherapy for cancer
- wasting, or severe weight loss, in people who may have cancer or AIDS
- neurological disorders, such as multiple sclerosis (MS).

Although some people smoke cannabis for therapeutic reasons, there are many researchers around the world who are currently trying to develop synthetic products that work in a similar way to cannabis. We use the term 'cannabinoids' to refer to pharmaceutical-quality drugs that act in the same way in the body as some substances in the cannabis plant, such as THC. Two examples of cannabinoids are nabilone, which is THC in a capsule and is available in the UK for medical uses, and dronabinol, which is synthetic THC, and is available in the US. At this time there are no cannabinoid drugs readily available in Australia.

It is very important to remember that cannabis and cannabinoids are useful to relieve symptoms of illnesses, but do not cure the underlying disease. Using cannabis for medical reasons is all about weighing up the pros and cons. There are a range of negative consequences associated with cannabis use, some of them linked to smoking the drug, others not. One of the most significant of these is that the drug is illegal. A person who uses cannabis for medical reasons and gets caught is not exempt from prosecution. These risks need to be acknowledged. However, if a person is dying from cancer, is in great pain and does not have long to live, and all the pharmaceutical drugs in the world have not made any difference, the possibility of some relief can make cannabis appear very attractive.

When Sid called to ask me questions about cannabis and its effects, I was immediately impressed by the older gentleman. He had been married to his wife, Mary, for over 50 years and for the past few years she had been extremely ill as a result of cancer. She had been bedridden for the past six months and in great pain. The doctors had tried every type of painkiller but none had been effective. The doctors said that she did not have much time to live and the best they could do was to keep her as comfortable as possible. Unfortunately they didn't seem to be doing a very good job of that.

Sid had heard about cannabis from the partner of a cancer sufferer who had experienced effective pain relief after smoking cannabis. Sid finally approached one of his grandsons and asked him to purchase the drug so he could see if it would work for his wife. He used it in a tea and saw an immediate beneficial effect on Mary and now desperately wanted to know more.

He told me that he could not buy the drug through his family anymore. He was well aware that the drug was illegal and did not want to expose any of his family members to the legal ramifications, but he did not know where to turn next. I referred him to some pro-cannabis websites that could possibly give him some information and wished him well.

Over six months later Sid called to tell me that Mary had died. He told me that the last few months of her life had been almost pain-free thanks to some cannabis that Sid had been able to purchase through a website which was set up to help people like him.

Sid had faced a major moral dilemma. He did not approve of illegal drugs and he was well aware of the legal risks that he was taking. He had read up on the health effects of cannabis, however, and felt that it was worth the risk to improve Mary's quality of life.

When you discuss this topic with your children there are a multitude of moral issues that come into play. For most parents, this conversation with your teenagers is not going to be as easy as 'cannabis is a medicine' or 'cannabis is illegal'. This is a complex area and one that can stimulate interesting debate and thought from all parties.

5
OTHER DRUGS

Almost every time I finish giving a presentation to a group of parents I get a mother or a father coming up to me wanting to speak about their own family experiences. Inevitably I hear the line: 'My kids are now twenty and eighteen and, thank God, they made it through adolescence without becoming involved with illegal drugs . . .'

I never have the heart to tell them that if their children are ever going to experiment with illicit substances, it is most likely to be in their twenties, after they have left home, and not in their teens.

The notion that illegal drug use is more likely to occur when kids are in high school is not supported by any evidence. The tabloid media has a great deal to answer for here. I can tell you that every time I am interviewed for a story on a drug I am usually asked 'How many young people use the drug?' or 'What is the youngest person you have heard of using the drug?' Even if you assure the journalist that this is a substance preferred by people in their twenties and we rarely see teenagers using it, you will inevitably find a headline declaring CHILDREN AS YOUNG AS 12 USING at the top of the article!

Even though it would appear that initiation into illicit drug use is starting earlier, for the vast majority of users we are still talking about a time after they have left school. The only real exception is cannabis, but as I've mentioned, cannabis use among young people has been dropping quite dramatically in recent years.

That said, it is still incredibly important that parents have conversations around illicit drug use and let their children know what their views are on the subject. Without a doubt the one drug that does need to be discussed with young Australians is ecstasy. Ecstasy use continues to increase in this country, and it is perceived by many young people as a fairly benign drug, particularly when compared to alcohol. Very little school-based drug education is provided in the area of ecstasy and parents should take every opportunity to talk about this increasingly popular substance. Thankfully all the evidence we have suggests that very few school-based young people have ever used ecstasy. But there is definitely an interest there, and if a teenager is exposed to the drug it is possible they may choose to experiment, particularly if they haven't been provided with any information to suggest why they shouldn't.

Always remember that you don't need to know everything about a drug to have a conversation with your child about it. If your child asks a question about a drug like ecstasy and you don't know the answer, the most powerful words you can use in response are: 'I don't know the answer. Let's find out together.'

This type of situation provides a wonderful opportunity for families to discover and learn new things, to discuss possible situations that may arise and develop strategies to cope with a wide variety of challenges that your adolescent may have to face in the future.

This chapter covers the main issues that are raised by young people and parents around drugs such as ecstasy, ice, LSD and those used in drink spiking. Hopefully the information provided will clear up a few of the myths that you or your child may believe to be true, as well as offering ways to start having positive conversations about what is an extremely controversial and complex issue.

• Can ecstasy really kill?

It surprises many that this question is so often asked by young people. Over the years there have been a number of high-profile ecstasy-related deaths of young Australians. The most well known of these occurred in October 1995 when a Sydney schoolgirl died after taking an ecstasy tablet at an inner-city nightclub. Her death resulted in community outrage about the use of ecstasy and changed government policy in the area. Why then, after so much widespread media attention, do so many young people doubt that deaths really occur?

An ecstasy-related death is rare, but it does happen. For the vast majority of people who use the drug, however, this is not their reality. Most ecstasy users have a pleasurable experience—that's why they continue to use the drug—and very few people have had direct contact with someone who has died after taking it. As a result, many people believe that ecstasy is harmless, or at least less harmful than other drugs.

It is difficult to say exactly how many ecstasy-related deaths have occurred in Australia over the years. When a death is reported users often look for other excuses for the incident, convincing themselves that it couldn't be ecstasy that caused it, it must have been other drugs or perhaps the person had a pre-existing condition. In many cases this is true—it is rare for a person to die due to ecstasy poisoning as MDMA (the substance people are actually after in a pill) is not a particularly toxic drug. However, poisonings have occurred and, no matter how much people may want to believe that ecstasy was not to blame, if the person hadn't taken the drug they would still be alive.

Unfortunately, people still believe that the majority of problems caused by ecstasy are due to impurities, i.e. the other substances that are found in a tablet. This is a myth—very rarely do we find that there are substances in ecstasy that are more toxic than MDMA. Although there are exceptions, the major problems that we continue to see with ecstasy are related to dehydration and overheating.

I was working in the medical tent at a large-scale event when we had a major incident. A young man and his girlfriend had bought several ecstasy tablets from their regular dealer. When they got to the rave they split one of the tablets in two and took half each. The young man had been using ecstasy for ten years. In all that time he had never experienced any severe problems associated with his drug use. He regarded himself as a responsible drug user and followed some basic 'rules' around not mixing drugs, taking regular breaks and making sure he was hydrated.

The couple were on the dance floor when the young man started to feel very hot. His body temperature soared and he became flushed and very uncomfortable. Knowing something was wrong he alerted his girlfriend and they left the floor. She fanned him, poured cold water over him and took him outside, where it was cooler. Nothing worked—in fact, he was getting hotter! They decided to seek help.

By the time they got to the medical tent he had lost consciousness. His body temperature was so high it was difficult to touch him. The medical staff acted quickly, using ice blankets to try to bring his temperature down, but nothing worked. An ambulance was called and he was rushed to hospital. Nobody in the tent expected him to survive. If he did, we expected that he would suffer brain damage due to his high temperature. Luckily that was not the case. By some miracle he survived and after a few days in hospital he recovered completely.

There was no explanation for his condition. His girlfriend took the other half of the pill and had no problems at all. The man was not a naïve user and the pill was not 'bad'. Sometimes these things just happen—drugs are unpredictable.

Apart from the unpredictable nature of drugs, another possible explanation is that there is no quality control when it comes to ecstasy manufacture. Unlike pharmaceutical drugs, where the contents are carefully monitored and regulated, an ecstasy pill can be very uneven in terms of the distribution of the active chemical.

One half of the pill could have far more MDMA (or other substance) than the other, resulting in one person getting a far greater dose.

Ecstasy, like any drug, can also attack weaknesses in the user. There have been cases where seemingly healthy young people use the drug and experience fits, strokes and heart attacks. Often these are people who have used the drug many times and have never had a bad experience. There is no apparent reason why these deaths occurred at that particular time.

You never know how a drug is going to affect you, and if you are going to use ecstasy give it the respect it deserves! You should never underestimate the risk associated with any drug.

• What are ecstasy testing kits and are they helpful?

Ecstasy testing kits have been available over the internet, as well as in some specialist stores in Australia, for some time. They are used primarily to test ecstasy tablets for the presence of MDMA.

These kits are basically reagent tests and are able to give some indication regarding a range of substances that may be present in an illicit substance. According to the websites for these products, the user drops some of the liquid provided in the kit onto a small scraping of the pill or powder. A pill which contains MDMA will quickly turn dark blue, purple or black, while other substances may turn yellow or green. If the substance contains amphetamines it will show orange or brown.

So what are these tests actually telling the user? Do they provide them with information that can be used to determine a certain degree of safety?

Well, no. It is important to be aware that an ecstasy tablet rarely contains only one substance. Often a tablet can contain many different substances, some of which are not even identifiable to the highly skilled analysts who work in government laboratories. Some of the substances that have been identified include a range of amphetamine-like substances such as MDEA, MDA, MBDB, DOB, PMA and a range of other stimulants, including ephedrine and caffeine. Ketamine and LSD have also been found in some ecstasy tablets.

These simple tests are, at best, able to identify one substance. Unfortunately many people using these kits identify MDMA and then incorrectly assume that this means the tablet is safe. There are two problems with this. First, MDMA is not a safe drug—as previously discussed, there are risks associated with its use, primarily around dehydration and overheating. Second, there may be other substances which were not even identified by the kit that are more harmful than MDMA.

I'm afraid there are no guarantees and no short cuts when it comes to drug use.

Shale and Lisa contacted me after a particularly nasty experience. Both in their late teens, the two young women used ecstasy fairly regularly. They were very involved in the dance scene and tried to keep up to date with drug information. They had heard about ecstasy testing kits from some of their friends and finally got the courage to buy one over the web. They had recently bought a number of pills that they were planning to use on their next big night out and were eager to test them out.

When they tested their pills they discovered that they had indeed purchased pills that contained MDMA, the substance you 'want' when you buy ecstasy. They were thrilled, believing the pills were definitely 'safe'.

When the night arrived they took the pills but were totally unprepared for what happened next. Believing the pills to be 'good ones', each of the girls took a whole tablet (something that neither had ever done before) and within an hour they were both terribly unwell. They had very high body temperatures and were suffering extreme nausea. In fact, Lisa vomited for almost an hour before one of the nightclub's security guards found her and took both her and Shale to see the medical team.

The medical team at the nightclub were worried about both her high temperature and her continual vomiting, and Lisa was eventually transferred to the accident and emergency department of the local hospital. After about an hour at the hospital she was allowed to go home, but the experience she had been through would change her attitude to drugs forever.

As I said, Lisa and Shale contacted me some time later. They had heard me on the radio and wanted to share their story so that others would not be lulled into a false sense of security as they were. They had seen the results of the ecstasy testing kit as some sort of 'seal of approval' and an indication of quality. They had been given a little bit of information and misread it.

An ecstasy testing kit can provide limited information. It is very useful if it successfully detects a poisonous substance, essentially warning potential users about the risks. Unfortunately some young people, particularly the very naïve, continue to believe that MDMA is a safe drug and that if they detect that substance then the pill must be okay.

Although ecstasy testing kits do provide some useful information to the person considering taking the pill, there are still lots of unknowns. There is no way of knowing all of the substances contained in the pill and how much of each there is, and most importantly, there is no chance that you could tell with any certainty what the contents (both identified and not identified) will do to you when you take it. Taking any drug is risky, and taking an illicit drug especially so, even when you have identified what some of its contents may be.

• What is a bad trip and how can you look after someone who is having one?

A 'trip' is a slang term for a drug experience, usually LSD or some other type of hallucinogenic drug, although some people talk about having bad trips on drugs like cannabis and alcohol. A hallucinogen is a substance that makes you think and feel things in a different way. That is, after you've used a hallucinogen your perception is altered; for example, you may look at your hand and think it looks larger, smaller, closer or further away than it really is—it may even start talking to you!

A bad trip is when the pleasant effects of a drug turn into a nasty and scary experience. Usually it begins as an overwhelming feeling of anxiety but in some cases the user starts to see things that they are very frightened of like spiders and snakes.

Bad trips usually happen for a reason. These can include using more of the drug than you are used to; trying to resist the effects of the drug because you are scared or can't relax; being in an unpleasant environment where you don't feel comfortable; and having problems weighing on your mind before you used the drug. Even people who have used drugs for a long time sometimes have a bad trip.

James was fifteen, and at the age when he loved to try new things. He lived on the north coast of New South Wales and had heard a lot about magic mushrooms. His older brother's friends had said that they were great fun and James was keen to try them.

One Saturday night his brother was able to organise a small amount of mushrooms for James and his friends to try. They each had some and within a short time they were all falling around the floor laughing at anything and everything. However it wasn't long before James's experience took a turn for the worse. He began to feel very anxious and strangely paranoid, convinced that his friends did not want him around them. Trying to push the feelings away, James ate more of the mushrooms.

The feeling became overwhelming and James became very scared. His friends tried to reassure him but to no avail—he was having a 'bad trip' and he would just have to 'ride the wave' until the effect of the hallucinogenic substances had worn off. Convinced that he was going to die and still refusing to accept his friends' help, James rolled into a foetal position and waited . . .

The best way to avoid a bad trip is to avoid taking a drug at all. Often a bad trip starts small and snowballs into rising feelings of anxiety, fear and paranoia. People who are having such an experience may appear withdrawn and quiet, or visibly upset and frightened. In extreme cases they may become wild and out of control. Often they will do exactly as James did and curl up into the foetal position.

This experience can make the person feel as if they are going insane or about to die. Sometimes they may find it difficult to breathe and it may trigger a full-blown panic attack.

The most important thing to remember in the midst of a bad trip is not to panic. If someone you know is having a bad trip, here are a few things you can do to lessen the impact and make them feel more comfortable:

- Change the environment. This can involve moving the person, altering the music that is playing or changing the lighting in the room. Never force anyone to do anything—remember, they are already paranoid. Gently encourage them to move into another room. Don't scare them any further.
- Reassure them that the reason they are feeling the way they do is because of what they have taken and the experience will end in time. They need to be told that they will be okay.
- Let them know the time. One of the side effects of using hallucinogens is the distortion of time and sufferers can feel that their bad trip is lasting forever. Letting them know how much time has really passed is extremely helpful and reassuring.
- Help them to relax by breathing with them. The fear that many people feel during a bad trip is often made worse by tensing up and trying to resist. If you can get them to 'let go' and relax it will make them feel better. Concentrating on good breathing technique will relax them and give them something to focus on.
- Never leave them alone. It is important for them to know that they are not by themselves, but at the same time, make sure that they have lots of space so they do not feel hemmed in.

• What drugs are most likely to be used in drink spiking and how can I protect myself from the crime?

Drink spiking is a crime we know little about and much of what is reported in the media is inaccurate. Drink spiking does happen and we know most about those spikings that led to another crime being committed, such as drug-assisted sexual assault or drug-assisted robbery.

People who believe that they have been the victim of drink spiking often say the same thing—'the night was a blank'. The drugs used in drink spiking are believed to be amnesic in effect, and therein lies one of the greatest problems when it comes to collecting good information about how often this crime is actually committed. People are often confused about exactly what happened and rarely report the crime until it is too late to collect vital information, including administering tests to tell what drugs have been used.

We do know that alcohol is the drug that is most likely to be used in drink spiking, although that is rarely reported.

While speaking to a group of fifteen- and sixteen-year-old young men about a range of drug issues, the subject of drink spiking came up. There was a range of questions about what drugs were used, how to prevent your drink being spiked and how to identify a potential drink spiker.

When they were informed that according to the best information we had, alcohol was the drug most likely to be used in spiking incidents, one of the young men, Justin, became very concerned.

Earlier in the discussion, Justin had expressed his disgust at the thought of drink spiking. How could anyone believe they had the right to put something into someone else's drink and get away with it? This was a serious crime and the people who were caught doing this should be punished to the full extent of the law. But when the subject of alcohol was added to the mix, Justin no longer saw it in the same way.

He took me to one side and informed me that he and his mates had occasionally bought a bottle of absinthe to take with them when they were having a big night out. Absinthe is a highly alcoholic drink, usually green in colour, which has recently seen an upsurge in popularity. When they joined up with a group of girls they knew later in the evening, they might add a shot of the extremely potent spirit to the unknowing females' drinks.

Justin was very worried that this could be regarded as drink spiking and tried desperately to defend his actions. In his words, he was 'only helping the girls to get as drunk as they wanted to be'. Although I tried to explain that secreting anything into someone else's drink with the purpose of making them more intoxicated was without a doubt 'drink spiking', Justin would not have it.

Drugs such as Rohypnol, ketamine and GHB are usually associated with drink spiking, but research has shown over and over again that these drugs, although routinely checked for, are rarely identified when someone is tested after an alleged spiking.

Realistically, any drink spiker worth their salt is not going to use a drug that can be easily identified. There have been cases in the media recently where perpetrators of this crime have been caught and the drugs they were using had previously never even been considered by authorities. Although we have amazing equipment, unless we know what we're looking for, we're never going to find it!

One of the great myths around drink spiking is that there are substances that are tasteless, odourless and impossible to detect. First of all, if this is true, why does cough medicine taste so bad? If there were drugs that were tasteless and odourless, pharmaceutical companies would be marketing them. At the very least, most drugs have a chemical taste to some degree, while others just taste plain revolting.

GHB (or fantasy, as it is sometimes known) is a drug that is often linked to drink spiking because it is said to be odourless and tasteless. Ask anyone who knows anything about this drug and they will tell you that this is simply not true. At the very least, 'true' GHB has a very salty taste, and at worst it has a very strong chemical smell and taste, making it almost impossible to disguise.

Young people need to know that if they taste anything unusual (generally salty or chemical tasting) or feel anything gritty in their drink, they should stop drinking immediately and let a friend know about their fears. Often the only way they wouldn't be able to identify that something had been placed in their drink is if they were already intoxicated.

Possibly the most important thing to remember is that someone who is sober is probably not going to be targeted by a spiker. Whatever drug is put into a drink will have much more of an effect if the victim is already affected by alcohol. If you are drinking alcohol, you are immediately a potential target for a drink spiker and should take precautions.

Drink spiking is usually considered to be a crime that is carried out by strangers. Most of the campaigns dealing with the issue warn about people lurking in bars and nightclubs waiting to slip something into your drink without you knowing. Interestingly, most of what we know about drink spiking does not match that scenario. In fact, most of the cases that have made it to court involve people who are known to the victim. Also, many of these spikings do not occur in bars and nightclubs. Instead, they take place in the home or some other place away from crowds. If you think about it; it would be much more difficult to drug someone in a crowded bar than in a party held at someone's home. If spiking was to take place in a venue, how would the offender be able to get the victim away from the club or pub without anyone noticing?

The myth that it is only strangers who carry out this crime is potentially dangerous as it leads some young people to take unnecessary risks. People you know, or have recently met, are just as likely to spike your drink as complete strangers, particularly if they are able to get you into a situation where you are on your own.

Rebecca was a fairly rebellious sixteen-year-old. She had just started seeing a much older boy and her mother, Bronwyn, was not happy about it. He seemed to be just as wild as Rebecca and, as a result, Bronwyn banned her daughter from going out with him. Not that Rebecca was going to listen to that . . .

Late on a Saturday night, after her mother had gone to bed, Rebecca scrambled out of her bedroom window and ran down the road to where her new boyfriend was waiting in his car. Without thinking she jumped into the passenger seat. It wasn't until the car had left her street that she realised there was someone in the back seat.

Her boyfriend introduced his best friend to Rebecca. She wasn't impressed about someone else coming out with them but there was little she could do. Their plans had been to go to a party across town so she thought that she would be able to ditch the 'third wheel' there. But they didn't seem to be travelling in the direction of the party.

They finally ended up parking near a reserve on the outskirts of town. Rebecca was told that they were going to have a few drinks together before moving on to the party. The young man in the back of the car handed Rebecca a bottle.

Rebecca took the bottle (which appeared to be a pre-mixed spirit) and had a swig of its contents. She immediately knew that something wasn't quite right. The drink appeared to have a salty taste and when she passed it to the young men, both refused to share it. She didn't really have any options; she was in a car with two young men, one of whom she didn't know, in a strange place and she now thought that she had been drugged in some way.

Rebecca doesn't remember too much after that, although she does recall feeling very drunk for a while, after which it all merges into one very unpleasant dream. When she woke up she found herself on her front lawn. The sun was just coming up and it took her some time to work out where she was and what had happened to her.

When she told her mother what had happened, Bronwyn immediately took her to the local hospital where she was tested for the presence of a range of drugs. There were no drugs detected.

Unfortunately there was evidence of sexual assault. They filed a police report and the young men were arrested, although neither of them was convicted of any charge due to the lack of evidence, since Rebecca had no memory of the incident whatsoever.

Here are some simple tips on how to avoid drink spiking from occurring:

- Always get your own drink. Watch it being poured.
- Don't leave your drink unattended.
- Don't taste anybody else's drink.
- Don't accept drinks from anyone else.

Drink spiking does happen. Make sure you look after yourself and look after your friends. If your friend seems drunk, or is acting out of character, but you know they haven't had that much to drink, there is the possibility that they may have been drugged. It is important that you take action immediately. If they tell you they think their drink may have been spiked it is important that you believe them.

Stay with them. Make sure you report the suspected crime to the authorities and, if possible, provide urine and blood samples to the police and ask that they be tested for traces of drugs. It is vital that this be done immediately after the suspected spiking.

So remember these things:

- Drink spiking does occur.
- If your drink is salty, chemical-tasting or gritty, stop drinking.
- Spiking is just as likely to occur in a home or party as it is in a nightclub or bar.
- It is more likely to be carried out by someone you know, or have recently struck up a friendship with, than a stranger.
- The drug most likely to be used is alcohol.
- If you are already intoxicated, you are more likely to be a target.

• Are we really in the middle of an 'ice epidemic'?

To understand the whole 'ice' issue, it is important to have some background information about amphetamines. Amphetamines—often referred to as 'speed'—are a group of stimulant drugs that increase central nervous system activity. These drugs can come in many different forms but are usually sold as a powder. The drug varies in colour from white to beige, orange and pink, and anywhere in between. It can also come in crystal form, tablets or even as a liquid.

One form of amphetamines is methamphetamine. Some people call the crystalline form of methamphetamine 'ice'. It may also be called by other names, such as 'crystal meth', 'crystal' and 'meth'. Speed and ice are similar drugs and have similar effects as they are from the same amphetamine family. However, ice may have more powerful effects because of its higher purity.

Methamphetamine has been an extremely hot topic in the Australian media for some time. Hardly a week goes past without some new story with a link to ice. We've had an 'ice storm' and 'ice babies', even ice supposedly being sold in lolly form to children (more of that on pages 156–158), and you can guarantee we're bound to have more of the same in the future.

Don't get me wrong, methamphetamine has become a significant drug issue within our community, particularly for frontline workers such as hospital emergency department staff and the police. However, the impression that this drug has permeated mainstream society and is reaching epidemic proportions in the general community is not supported by any real evidence; in fact, all the evidence we have would suggest that use has been going down. What we have experienced in the last few years has been the emergence of new forms of methamphetamine becoming more widely available on the illicit drug market. This has not necessarily made the pool of drug users any larger, but it has led to changes in patterns of use among existing drug users.

For a long time methamphetamine usually available in Australia was the 'salt' form of the drug ('speed'). However, new, more pure forms of the drug have emerged, like ice. With an average purity of around 80 per cent, it is no surprise that it is the crystalline form that has proved popular with illicit drug users. With the quality of street drugs traditionally low, we have seen a range of drug users (such as injecting drug users and ecstasy users) experiment with a high-quality drug that is readily available and reasonably priced. Essentially, drug users have found a drug that gives them 'more bang for their buck'.

However, this effect comes at a price. Increasing numbers of users have become dependent on methamphetamine and there has been an increase in related problems (including psychosis and other mental health issues). This has placed increasing demands on service providers and it is usually these workers that we have seen interviewed on current affairs programs.

Unfortunately, while concern continues to grow around methamphetamine, we lose sight of other problems. As is often the case with the media, there is rarely any context given to issues. Methamphetamine use does not exist in a vacuum. Ice users nearly always use a range of other drugs, with many of the more serious cases, particularly those identified in media stories, also being heroin-dependent. This is rarely, if ever, spoken about and thus the general community is given only half the story. The impact that alcohol may have had on the ice user is often ignored too.

Methamphetamine use is a significant issue in the Australian community and needs to be addressed. However, we need to ensure that we put it into context and do not focus on it to the exclusion of other, potentially more serious problems in our society. For the majority of parents the 'ice epidemic' is a non-issue. It is important to discuss the stories that we see and hear in the media but remember to stay focused on those issues that are far more likely to have an impact on your teenagers, such as alcohol.

6
WADING THROUGH SOME URBAN MYTHS

An urban myth or legend can be defined as a second-hand story that is told as true, which is likely to be framed as a cautionary tale. It generally involves one or more unusual events that supposedly happened to a real person. The person sharing the story usually knows of the person it happened to, or knows someone who knows them. We've all been told an outrageous story which ends with the words: 'It's true—it really happened to my mother's hairdresser's sister!'

For a long time these stories were passed from one person to another through conversation. Nowadays we have the internet. Warning emails on a variety of topics regularly do the rounds, but drugs appear to be one of the most popular subjects. These emails feed into the natural fear that many people, particularly parents, have around drugs. They often have limited knowledge on the topic and are greatly concerned about their children becoming involved with the drug culture, so when one of these emails arrives in their in-box, it simply reinforces their existing fears. And because they are often received from friends they know well and trust, they are believed and passed on!

There is also a great deal of drug folklore that exists among young drug users. This usually comprises bits of information on a range of topics that has spread from person to person. For many teenagers, this folklore relates to personal safety.

Young people, like everybody else in our society, obtain much of their drug information from pretty unreliable sources, particularly their friends. But as it is passed from one person to another, the information is subtly changed, with people often adding their own interpretation or interesting sideline. No matter how innocent the information is at the beginning of the chain, by the time it reaches the end, it now contains a couple of swear words and a bizarre sexual act!

This chapter examines some of the urban myths and folklore that exist in our society and aims to provide some more accurate information on the topics discussed.

• Is it true that drug pushers are now targeting very young children by adding strawberry flavouring to their products, or selling tattoos with LSD on them?

Stories about drug manufacturers and dealers targeting very young children have been around for many years. The 'Blue Star' tattoo myth is possibly the most famous of these and goes back to 1980, although some say the story was circulating earlier than that.

In the past the story usually hit the headlines after a local school or police station received a copy of a flyer warning that LSD-soaked tattoos were being given away to children in local schoolyards. Nowadays it is usually an email message that is received by a concerned citizen who alerts the local media.

The information conveyed in the message can vary but usually explains that the LSD can be absorbed through the skin by handling the tattoos. The tattoos are the same size as postage stamps and have been designed to attract very young people by depicting cartoon characters. It goes on to say that these drugs are known to act very quickly and some are laced with strychnine. In fact, it warns, many children have already died from accidental ingestion of these tattoos. The message is usually signed by a representative of a well-known government agency or hospital, and to the naïve reader it appears to be quite genuine. Those receiving the alert are asked to forward the email urgently to as many people as possible.

Of course, the information contained in the email is all completely untrue. In fact, it simply doesn't make sense. Why would drug manufacturers and dealers target the very young in the first place? They are most probably in the business to make money and would be looking for markets where they are able to do that without too much work. Primary school-aged children do not usually have cash to spend on drugs. The whole idea of the dealers trying to get the very young 'hooked' on a substance so that they have a ready-made market in the future is quite ridiculous. How long are they prepared to wait?

The concept of the 'drug pusher' is also quite problematic. The reality is that there is already a demand for illegal drugs and most people who sell them do not need to promote their product. Indeed, most dealers would prefer to have a small number of regular 'clients' rather than a large number that they don't know particularly well. Having too many people knowing what you do increases your risk of getting caught.

The 'Blue Star' myth has been around for longer than most mainly because it has been regularly updated (in the 1980s the alerts claimed Mickey Mouse was depicted on the tattoos, in the 90s it became Bart Simpson) and also because LSD is sold in the form of small paper squares, usually illustrated with a design of some sort, including cartoon characters. However, LSD is not available in either a tattoo or transfer form.

More recently, mainly due to the increased use of methamphetamine around the world, particularly in the US and Australia, we have seen a new urban myth hit the headlines. Media stories quoted US drug agencies warning Australians to brace for a new wave of strawberry-flavoured amphetamines specifically designed to appeal to juvenile tastebuds. These stories were accompanied by email alerts sent around the country warning parents to be on the lookout for this new form of the drug, which was once again being used by 'drug pushers' to target their children.

The flavoured drug, known as 'strawberry ice', was apparently already proving popular with young users in the United States. According to these sources, strawberry flavouring and some reddish food colouring was added to the mix during the manufacturing process.

So what do we know about 'strawberry ice'? According to websites that deal explicitly with investigating urban myths, this story is partially true. It started to do the rounds in early 2007 after some seizures of red methamphetamine were made in a number of states across the US. Drug Enforcement Agency (DEA) agents were reported as saying that the drug resembled Pop Rocks (a lolly that fizzes in the mouth) and that it was another example of the depths to which 'evil drug dealers' would stoop.

The problem with this story is that there is no evidence to support the claim that there had been flavouring added to the drug. Yes, it may have been brightly coloured (which could have been due to the manufacturing process and the chemicals used and not, in fact, a marketing ploy), but did it taste like strawberries? No evidence of any taste tests exists. It was all rumour and 'someone telling someone something that someone else had told them'. Naturally, concerned parents forwarded the email alert to their friends believing that they were doing the right thing.

So what should you do if you receive one of these emails? How do you know if the information is accurate or not?

My best advice is to contact the source. These emails usually contain a quote from a law enforcement officer or a hospital representative stressing the urgency of the situation. Before you pass the email on, spend a moment or two trying to get in contact with the person quoted in the story. These email warnings are dangerous. If you do receive one, or any other drug warning by email, please don't forward it on before attempting to check its authenticity.

• Do energy drinks increase the effect of alcohol when you use them as a mixer?

The issue of energy drinks is an interesting one because both parents and their children ask questions about them, but from very different perspectives. Young people usually want to know if mixing one of these energy drinks with alcohol is likely to make you more drunk—that is, does it increase the effect of alcohol? Parents, on the other hand, want to know about the risks associated with drinking these popular beverages. Let's deal with the risks first.

Energy drinks have become increasingly popular over the past few years and are marketed very heavily to young people. In the advertising that promotes these products we are told that these drinks will give us an extra energy boost and there is the suggestion that there is something contained within the drink that you are not going to find elsewhere. Some products do have additional ingredients (such as guarana), but in most cases caffeine and sugar are the active ingredients which give these drinks their supposed 'boost'.

Caffeine is without a doubt the world's stimulant of choice. Most adults consume about 200 milligrams of caffeine on a given day—that's equivalent to about five cans of Coke, four cups of tea, a large bar of chocolate or two cups of instant coffee. If you like your coffee more upmarket, you may be consuming much, much more. Some coffees from the well-known franchises contain an amazing 550 milligrams of caffeine. Just one cup will put you up around the level that many health experts believe is of concern.

In small to moderate amounts, caffeine may have the beneficial effects of stimulating alertness and decreasing drowsiness. However, when consumed in large amounts, caffeine can cause a variety of negative side effects such as nervousness, insomnia, muscle twitching, rapid heart rate, irritability and trouble concentrating. Most experts believe that there is little risk of harm when a person consumes less than 600 milligrams of caffeine a day. If you can keep your caffeine intake level below that you need not worry about the negative health effects. If you are consuming more, you should start to seriously consider cutting back.

Of course, we would hope that a child's daily intake of caffeine was much lower. I used to hate it when my father said this, but 'in my day' it was very rare to see young people, even teenagers, drink much coffee. I find it quite confronting when I arrive at a school in the morning and see teenage girls being dropped off with a cup of coffee from the local cafe in their hand. It's interesting to note the concern that some parents have regarding energy drinks and their caffeine levels, while at the same time they virtually ignore the fact that their child is regularly consuming a range of other caffeine-based products, including coffee.

So how much caffeine is your child likely to consume when they have one of these energy drinks? If you believe the hype, you would think that the product is almost all caffeine, however the reality is quite different. Yes, there are some energy drinks that contain up to two or three times as much caffeine as a cup of instant coffee, but on average they contain about 80 milligrams, or slightly less than your morning cuppa.

Of great concern to many parents are the deaths linked to these drinks. Over the years it has been reported that a number of young people who have consumed quite large amounts of these products have subsequently died. Each one of these deaths is a tragedy and parents do need to be concerned, but it is important to note that it would appear each of these young people had a pre-existing condition and it is likely there would have been a similar outcome if they had drunk a great deal of coffee or tea. Like any drug, it is not necessarily the use of the drug that has caused the problem, but the abuse of it.

The problem with suggesting that these drinks have special or unusual properties is that our young people pick up on this and the product then seems much more attractive. It also leads to a great deal of mythology building up around the products.

Tim was a high-achieving year twelve student who was just about to start his final exams. He had been working hard and staying up late but wanted that extra boost to get him through the final few weeks. He was not interested in illegal drugs such as amphetamines and had been warned by teachers earlier in the year about the dangers of using over-the-counter caffeine medications. However, he had heard through some friends that the use of certain energy drinks improved memory and the ability to study. When I visited his school he approached me to ask if these products would indeed help him to study and whether there were any side effects.

This area is one which the energy drink manufacturers have leapt on. Some of the advertising for these products highlights the supposed positive effect that they can have on memory and learning. However, whether the drinks—and caffeine itself—can live up to this promise is another question. Some studies have suggested that small amounts of caffeine might increase alertness and short-term memory. However, other studies have shown that too much caffeine may actually have the reverse effect, such as interfering with the ability to focus and to easily recall information—not exactly desirable when preparing for exams. My advice to Tim was to avoid energy drinks and caffeine as an aid to study—although there could be some short-term benefits if a small amount of caffeine was con-sumed, he was most probably getting that from other things he was drinking and eating throughout the day. Too much caffeine could result in a range of problems, particularly the inability to sleep, and simply wasn't worth the risk.

There are risks associated with energy drinks but we do need to be careful not to overstate them. It would appear that most of these risks are associated with inappropriate caffeine intake. Too much caffeine can lead to unpleasant effects, whether your child drinks energy drinks, coffee or tea—so make sure that when you talk to your child about caffeine, you talk about the range of products that contain the drug. It could also be a great opportunity to examine your own caffeine use and whether you are consuming more than you should.

Parental concern about these products, combined with incredibly clever marketing by the manufacturers, has ensured that young people have a real interest in energy drinks. As I have already said, there are a great many myths about the amazing qualities of these drinks—including the idea that mixing them with alcohol will get you more drunk!

If you go to any nightclub or bar across the country, it is not unusual to see energy drink promotions taking place. These promotions usually involve beautiful young women moving through the establishment providing free samples of their product, either by itself or mixed with a spirit, most often vodka. Energy drinks are now regarded by many as the ideal mixer, and over time the belief that they somehow increase the effect of alcohol has developed.

So what do we know about the effect of the mix? Does it really have some strange magical properties?

In recent times there has been a number of studies that have examined this claim and it would appear that the effect can be explained very simply. Alcohol is a depressant, and one of the potential barriers to risky drinking is its depressant effects—that is, you start to feel drunk and sleepy and you stop. When you add a stimulant to the mix, such as caffeine, a person might be less aware of the effects of the alcohol and thus able to drink more.

Although these effects seem positive to young people, there are risks to this type of drinking. Without the barrier of the depressant effect, yes, you can drink more, but you also put yourself at greater risk of something going wrong. One study showed that those who mixed alcohol with energy drinks were more likely to be involved in a traffic accident or be the victim of a sexual assault, simply because they were unaware of how drunk they really were.

It is important to remember that even though you have had the stimulant (the caffeine in the energy drink), you are still drunk in terms of motor coordination, visual reaction times and blood alcohol concentration. The feeling of being drunk may be masked but you are still intoxicated. Put really simply, what you are doing to your body is putting your foot on the accelerator and the brake at the same time—it doesn't know what to do and that's when things can go wrong!

When you talk to your child about energy drinks and their risks make sure they are aware that the body responds to certain drugs to protect itself. When you're getting too drunk, your body slows down for a reason—if you try to artificially keep yourself going and ignore the messages your body is sending you, you are asking for trouble.

• Do illegal drugs sometimes contain things like laundry powder, bleach and ground glass?

Many people, including many drug users, believe that illegal drugs are often 'cut' with a variety of dangerous substances. These can range from products found in the laundry cupboard, such as detergent and bleach, through to rat poison, kitty litter and ground glass. There is also a belief that sometimes other, more dangerous illicit drugs are added, either to add to the effect or to get the unsuspecting user 'hooked' on the other substance. This particularly applies to ecstasy, with many users believing that some pills contain heroin (this supposed phenomenon is often referred to as 'smacky E's'). Cannabis users will talk of hearing that the plant is sprayed with other substances.

There is little evidence to support these beliefs. Before we look into the facts behind these myths, it is important to examine why these beliefs may exist in the first place.

First, it is commonly believed that little care is taken during the manufacturing process. We tell young people that drugs such as speed and ecstasy are manufactured in 'backyard laboratories' and, as a result, that any products could be used in the mix. Second, we constantly reinforce the fact that people involved in the manufacture and supply of drugs are capable of just about anything, and so it seems reasonable to believe that they would do incredibly irresponsible things like this.

In reality, if manufacturers did start to include things like rat poison in their mix, we would very quickly see the results and they would very quickly lose business! Although the labs used to make illicit drugs are not of the same quality as those used by pharmaceutical companies, it is highly unlikely that the chemists have boxes of rat poison hanging around that could accidentally fall into the mix. Without a doubt, organised crime is unscrupulous when it comes to increasing profits, and they're not really going to care about the misery that their products could inflict on the users. However, one thing everyone needs to remember is that the manufacturers and dealers want repeat business. If they were making and selling products that contained some of the things that are often discussed, their business would soon dry up.

Drugs that are seized by police are routinely tested both here and overseas. There is a great deal of forensic evidence available and many of the substances discussed have never been found. Drugs definitely have things added to them to improve profit margins, but usually these products are fairly benign and may include paracetamol, caffeine, glucose, lactose and other sugars. Bicarbonate of soda and Epsom salts have also been found. Of course, if you're talking about pills and tablets, a variety of starch and gums are also used to bind the drug together.

Unfortunately, urban myths like this are sometimes picked up and result in media reports and a wider belief that there is some basis in fact to the stories.

Many years ago a story ran in newspapers across the country about ecstasy being tested and found to contain ground glass. The story originated from a press release based on information from an article in a South-east Asian newspaper. Someone had found the article while on holiday and had brought it back to Australia.

To this day I still get questions about glass in ecstasy. The myth has been around for years and there is no evidence to support it. The story even attempts to explain why glass would be used: to make tiny cuts in the stomach to enable the ecstasy to enter the bloodstream faster, so the user will feel the effect of the drug more quickly.

When it comes to lacing drugs with other illicit substances in an attempt to entice naïve young people to start using them, it is important to consider one important thing—the cost. Drugs are expensive, and it just doesn't make any economic sense for drug manufacturers or suppliers to add other costly substances to their products in the hope that the unsuspecting user may get hooked on it in the future.

I should also emphasise once again that drugs are routinely tested and if some of these substances had been discovered we would know about it fairly quickly.

My greatest concern about this myth is that it diverts attention from the very real issue that the drug the user intended to buy is itself potentially dangerous. One of my pet hates is when you hear the police talking about a 'bad batch' of drugs currently available on the streets. This implies that there are 'good batches' available. Talking about adulterants, whether they be legally available products or illegal substances, reinforces the myth among drug users that the only real harm associated with their drug of choice relates to issues of purity. All drugs are risky and although the harms are different for different drugs and different people, they are real and our young people need to be aware of them.

It is important to let young people know that there is no way of being certain what is in any illicit substance—no matter what anyone says. Stories about drugs containing all types of weird and wonderful things such as rat poison and kitty litter are just that: stories. We need to make sure that we don't get carried away worrying about potentially dangerous adulterants that could have been added to the mix. When we do that we lose sight of the incredibly important message that what they are intending to buy is risky in itself.

• Does mixing over-the-counter painkillers with alcohol (or cola) have a 'special' effect?

There are several urban myths based around combining commonly available substances for a much more pronounced effect. The one that is best known (and has been around the longest) is that mixing any cola-based drink with aspirin will get you high—it was even mentioned in the popular movie *Grease*. Nowadays, however, young people are far more likely to talk about mixing painkillers with alcohol instead of cola drinks.

When you trawl the websites that are dedicated to busting urban myths it is interesting to see some of the things that the combination of cola (or alcohol) and over-the-counter painkillers is supposed to do. It is said, for example, to act as an aphrodisiac, kill you instantly or cure a hangover.

It's really no surprise that these sorts of stories do the rounds. Adolescence is a time for experimentation and for pushing the boundaries. There are so many things that young people are 'not meant to do' during this time and this includes using readily available pharmaceutical products inappropriately. When they hear stories about particular products having some bizarre effects when mixed together, it should come as no surprise that some of the more adventurous teenagers are going to try it.

So what do we know about paracetamol? Paracetamol is a simple painkilling medicine used to relieve mild to moderate pain and fever, and is the active ingredient in a whole range of capsule and tablet products. Despite its widespread use for over 100 years, we still don't fully understand how paracetamol works. However, it is thought that it works by reducing the production of some compounds in the brain and spinal cord which are produced by the body in response to injury and certain diseases. One of their actions is to sensitise nerve endings so that when an injury is stimulated it causes pain (most probably to prevent us from causing further harm to the area). As paracetamol reduces the production of these nerve-sensitising prostaglandins, it is thought it may increase our pain threshold, so that although the injury remains, we can feel it less.

Paracetamol is a fairly safe drug and, like the ads say, when used as directed it is not likely to cause any problems. However, if it is mixed with a powerful drug like alcohol is it likely to cause any serious health effects?

Well, first of all it is important to debunk the myth that this combination is going to result in some magical effect. There is no evidence to indicate that mixing paracetamol with alcohol (or cola) will do anything that could be perceived as positive. In fact, it is just the reverse.

First of all, we really don't know how much paracetamol the young people use when they play with this mix. Unfortunately, what we see so often with this type of myth is that after they have tried it out and there isn't any reaction, there is every likelihood that they will increase the amount so as to get an effect—if one doesn't do the job, maybe three will! It is extremely important that young people are aware that an overdose of paracetamol is very dangerous and is capable of causing serious damage to the liver and kidneys. You should start teaching your children from a very early age that they should never exceed the dose stated on a packet of over-the-counter or prescribed medication under any circumstances. Medical assistance should be sought immediately in the event of a paracetamol overdose, even if the person who has taken them feels well, because of the risk of delayed, serious liver damage.

Together, alcohol and paracetamol can be damaging to the liver and young people need to be told that this is a very risky activity. Discussing urban myths and how they begin can be a great conversation starter between you and your child. There are many websites dedicated to 'busting' these myths and many of them relate to drugs and drug use.

All parents are encouraged to try to make their children 'critical thinkers'. When they access information from any source, it is vital that they assess where the information is coming from, why it is being provided to them and whether there are any underlying agendas at play. This sort of critical thinking is best practised when watching tabloid television programs or reading gossip magazines. Even our most well-respected outlets are capable of 'getting it wrong'. So teaching our children this skill is vital. The more you practise this sort of analysis the greater the chance that your kids will reject much of the mythology that has developed around drugs and drug use.

• Does drinking milk before you drink alcohol really line your stomach? What about eating bread to sober you up?

One of the most popular 'tips' passed down from generation to generation has been that if you are planning on drinking alcohol you should make sure you line your stomach beforehand. There are many suggestions of what to use, but the most popular has always been a glass of milk. The reasons for doing this may vary—some people say that it will prevent a hangover, while others just believe that it will make the alcohol experience more pleasant.

It is important to remember that, unlike food, alcohol does not have to be digested before it can be absorbed into the bloodstream. Alcohol molecules are small and pass into the bloodstream quickly and easily. Some alcohol is immediately absorbed through the wall linings of the stomach, while the rest moves into the small intestine. All in all, alcohol makes its way through the digestive system pretty rapidly. However, on its way it can cause problems.

One of the major problems is that alcohol irritates the lining of the stomach. When it becomes irritated the stomach secretes a protective mucus and gastric juices. These juices don't affect the alcohol that much, but they do dilute its concentration in the stomach and can also delay the stomach emptying as it would usually. This can lead to stomach aches, nausea or vomiting. If your stomach is empty when you drink, the irritation will most probably be worse. Food, particularly those foods full of protein, such as milk, meat or eggs, appear to protect the stomach lining by slowing down the absorption of alcohol because the stomach has to break it down with gastric juice to start the process of digestion.

So it would appear that eating a small meal or consuming, at the very least, a glass of milk before you drink alcohol could help prevent things from turning nasty.

However, over time this message has been warped and has, on occasion, led to potentially life-threatening situations.

Seventeen-year-old Gary and fifteen-year-old Rosa had been seeing each other for a couple of weeks. They were going to a party on Saturday night and Rosa had invited her best friend, Liza, to join them.

The night was great fun, they all had a bit to drink, but Gary was definitely way ahead of the girls. He had been playing drinking games with his mates and he was now feeling pretty unwell. Rosa and Liza walked him out of the party and were heading home when they realised he wasn't going to make it. He was drifting in and out of consciousness and soon he passed out under a tree in a park.

Liza made several attempts to convince Rosa that they needed to call an ambulance or at least an older friend who could drive. Rosa refused and got increasingly angry with Liza as she believed that she could look after her boyfriend.

She had heard through friends that if you fed someone bread when they were drunk it would sober them up. This belief was so popular among Rosa's classmates that many of them even took slices of bread with them if they planned to drink. Rosa was one of those young people who believed in being prepared—she had bread in her bag! She started to feed Gary small pieces. Of course Gary found it extremely difficult to even open his mouth, let alone chew and swallow the bread, but Rosa persisted and gradually had fed him a whole slice.

By this time Liza had seen enough. She moved away from the pair and called an ambulance. Within minutes help arrived on the scene and found Rosa in tears, holding Gary in her arms. He was now blue and unconscious. The ambulance crew asked what had happened then swung into action, quickly removing a large amount of unchewed bread from the back of the young man's throat, where it had been slowly but surely choking him.

Gary survived, but only just. The ambulance crew told Rosa that if they had arrived just a few minutes later Gary would have choked on the bread that she had force-fed him.

Rosa's strategy of using bread to sober someone up is like any drug myth; most likely originating from accurate information, over time the content of the message had changed as it had been passed from one person to the next. It is not hard to see that it most probably comes from the message that eating something before you drink could prevent a bad experience but the potential damage this myth, and others like it, can cause is immense.

Interestingly, I have been to a number of schools in recent times where the bread and eating myth has evolved yet again. Young people are now saying that if you get home after a big night out the best way to prevent a hangover is to eat as much bread as you possibly can before you go to sleep. I have spoken to young people who have tried to consume as much as a loaf of bread before going to bed in an attempt to avoid a pounding headache the next day. This would be funny if it wasn't for the choking risk that these teenagers face if they haven't chewed and swallowed the bread properly.

The message we need to give teenagers is that although friends want to keep you safe, the information that they give you is not always correct. Always check out any information your friends give you as thoroughly as you can.

• Is the saying 'beer then grass, you're on your arse; grass then beer, you're in the clear' really true?

Without a doubt this is the number one question asked by young men in relation to illicit drugs. Maybe it's because they like to say the rhyme in front of their peers—it definitely gets a laugh—but it is important to remember that, not including tobacco, the most common 'mix' of drugs among young people in Australia is cannabis and alcohol. (For more information on young people and the use of these substances, see chapters 2–4.)

People who mix cannabis and alcohol say they do it to get more 'wasted' or 'out of it', or that they use the second drug to increase the effects of the first. One of the greatest problems that people appear to experience when they mix these two drugs is 'greening out'. This refers to the situation where, for reasons that we don't understand and cannot predict, people feel physically sick after smoking cannabis. They might go pale or even 'green'; they can feel sweaty and dizzy; they experience nausea and might even throw up.

So what about the old saying—does the order in which the drugs are taken have any impact on their effect?

Although the effects are not totally predictable, it does seem that you're more likely to have a bad reaction if you drink then smoke than if you smoke then drink. Many people say that greening out is more likely to happen if they have a smoke after they've been drinking. Some evidence suggests that when you have alcohol in your blood, you absorb THC (the part of cannabis that gets you stoned) faster. So you might end up having what is a normal amount of cannabis for you, but it has a much stronger effect than if you hadn't been drinking.

On the other hand, there is research to suggest that smoking cannabis can actually slow the absorption of alcohol, reducing the effects you feel from the alcohol. So it would appear that the old saying is correct to a point. However, it needs to be remembered that using one drug is risky, and mixing two drugs together greatly increases the risk of something going terribly wrong, no matter what the rhyme says.

• Is it true that one of the drugs used in drink spiking sterilises the victim?

At some time or another I am sure you've received an email from a friend you trust warning about some terrible new trend. Many times these involve drugs—ecstasy that contains glass and

LSD-soaked tattoos are just two that have already been covered in this chapter.

Another of these email hoaxes deals with a drug called 'Progesterex'. Here is a version of the email that I received in 2007:

> Please advise your daughters and send to as many people as possible—this is very tragic. On Saturday night a woman was taken from a nightclub by five men who, according to hospital and police reports, gang raped her before dumping her. She was unable to remember the events of the evening, but tests later confirmed the repeat rapes along with traces of Rohypnol in her blood, with Progesterex, which is essentially a small sterilisation pill which vets use to sterilise large animals.
>
> Rumour has it that Progesterex is being used together with Rohypnol, the date rape drug. Progesterex, which dissolves in drinks just as easily, means that the victim doesn't conceive from the rape and the rapist needn't worry about having a paternity test identifying him months later.
>
> The drug's effects are not temporary. They are permanent! Any female who takes it will never be able to conceive. The bastards can get this drug from anyone who is in vet school or any university. It's that easy.
>
> Please forward this to everyone you know, especially girls. Be careful when you're out, and don't leave your drink unattended. Guys, please inform all your female friends and relatives. Girls, keep your drinks safe at all times, and men, look after the girls you're with.
>
> Please pass this on to all your friends and family . . . Thank you.

There are many versions of this story but they usually involve a young woman being sexually assaulted by an unknown assailant. Tests later reveal traces of Progesterex in her blood. This one even adds the drug Rohypnol to the story, just to give it a little more authenticity.

It is, of course, a hoax, and the only reason for its existence appears to be to frighten young women. Progesterex doesn't exist! There's no mention of it anywhere in medical or scientific literature.

Legitimate drug warnings are incredibly important, however it's equally important to separate fact from fiction. As I've said before, if you receive this or any other warning by email, check out the facts carefully before forwarding it.

7

THOSE REALLY TOUGH QUESTIONS NO ONE WANTS TO ANSWER

I've left this batch of questions till last for a very good reason—they're pretty tough to answer!

So many parents tell me that they simply weren't prepared for the challenges that came with parenthood. Although the joys of having children far outweigh the difficulties (at least most of the time), there are always some issues which, no matter how many parenting books you've read, videos you've watched or lectures and classes you've attended, you have no idea how to respond to appropriately.

When it comes to drug issues, I'm most often surprised by those parents who actually experimented themselves as youngsters. One thing they never thought about when they were having a quick puff of a bong on a Saturday night during their university years was what they were going to tell their kids about their drug use in twenty years' time!

The first question in this section is one that you will almost inevitably be asked by your child at some time. For that reason, it's a good idea to work out in advance what you are going to say. In my experience, giving an unplanned response can lead to lies being told and this can be very damaging to a parent–child relationship.

Most parents claim they never want to make the same mistakes their own parents made. These perceived mistakes can centre around the quality of the relationship they have with their children, issues around rules and boundaries (e.g. not being as strict as their parents) or ensuring they provide their kids with more opportunities in a wide range of areas (e.g. education, music lessons, and so on). But all a parent's best intentions can go out the window when their child is suspected of—or, worse still, found to be—using illegal drugs.

All the ideals you had about communicating in a positive way, never shouting or punishing your children in an inappropriate manner, can count for nothing when you come across a bag of cannabis or an ecstasy pill at the bottom of your child's sock drawer. Panic, fear and then anger are the usual responses, and when those emotions are running high, common sense and reason do not prevail.

Although reading through the issues relating to finding an illicit drug in your child's room can never prepare you for the reality of that situation, hopefully it will give you something to think about and possibly discuss with your teenager. Knowing the facts about drug use and the risk of addiction can also help to allay some fears you may have.

I've said it before and I'll say it again—there is no rule book when it comes to being a parent. This chapter does not attempt to give you all the answers to the complex questions it raises. Rather, the information provided is designed to start you thinking about possible positive responses you may use in the future that are based on your family values and beliefs.

• What should I tell my child if they ask me if I ever used illegal drugs?

Most parents do not have a problem answering this question as, although the media would love to tell you that most people have experimented with illegal drugs, the opposite is true. The one illicit drug that is most likely to have been used by Australian parents is cannabis, but that is still only a third of the population. Most Australians (two-thirds of them) have not used the drug.

However, for those parents who have experimented with illicit drugs in their youth, this is a question they will dread—and it will almost certainly be raised at some stage during their child's teenage years. When it is, parents have one of three choices—they can tell the truth, they can avoid the question and hope it goes away, or they can lie through their teeth! It really is a dilemma.

Unfortunately, it is also becoming an issue for a growing number of parents who still occasionally dabble with a range of substances. Over the last decade there is evidence to suggest that we are seeing drug-using 'careers' stretching—that is, some people continue to use for longer periods of time, not stopping in their late twenties as is usually the case, but continuing to use into their forties and even fifties. This is particularly true for cannabis. While this is not a large number of people, it does appear to be a growing group.

Every parent will need to deal with this question in their own way, in a manner appropriate to their family. Below are stories of families in three very different circumstances telling how the parents have dealt with their particular situation. The stories also tell how the children in these families have responded. These are not necessarily representative—it is important to note that another parent could use exactly the same strategy and get a completely different outcome—but these case studies do illustrate that teenagers respond in a variety of ways, something which might help you when deciding on your own approach.

Nicole, a mother of three, was a big party girl back in the late 1980s and early 90s. Together with her then boyfriend, now husband, Peter, she was among the first generation of regular ecstasy users, who attended large dance parties and inner-city nightclubs. As well as ecstasy, she also used a variety of other drugs, including cannabis, speed and LSD. She says that she would find it difficult to estimate how much ecstasy she took during that period of her life, but she always knew that when she got married and made the decision to have children she would stop using—and that is exactly what she did.

Her eldest daughter, Hannah, is now fifteen years old and is beginning to ask questions about her parents' partying years. Nicole is now wondering how to talk to her teenage daughter about her drug use. Should she tell the truth, avoid the subject, or simply lie and say that it never happened?

She decided to lie. In fact, she has become hardline when it comes to the messages she gives to her children about drugs. As far as Nicole is concerned, drugs are dangerous and she doesn't want her children to use them.

'If I found out that Hannah was experimenting with any drug I would be horrified. I know it sounds hypocritical, particularly with my history, but as I've got older I've become more and more worried about my children and drugs. Maybe it's because I know so much more about them and the risks involved with their use. I simply don't want my children to use.'

The effect that this hardline attitude has had on Hannah is interesting. A bright girl who is doing very well at school, she told me that illegal drugs are not a part of her life, although she has just got into the party scene and drinks alcohol occasionally— something her mother frowns on.

'I would never talk about drugs with Mum and Dad,' she told me. 'Mum has made it very clear how she feels and often talks about people she knew who took drugs and got into real trouble. I can't even imagine what she would do if I did try drugs and she ever found out.'

Unfortunately, Nicole's attitude towards drugs appears to have caused a real communication barrier between her and her daughter.

'I have a friend who I think has a problem with drinking,' confessed Hannah. 'She drinks every weekend and I do worry about her. I'd love to be able to talk to Mum about it but I wouldn't dare. I couldn't trust her to keep it secret and not tell my friend's mum. In so many other ways I have a great relationship with Mum but I wouldn't even try to talk to her about this—she would just overreact and hit the roof.'

When asked whether she thought either of her parents had ever used drugs in the past Hannah was shocked at the suggestion.

'No way! Maybe Dad tried cannabis but definitely not Mum. If she did, I think I would be very angry—she is so anti-drug—I don't think I would trust her again. I definitely wouldn't believe anything she said about drugs!'

What is difficult to fathom with Nicole and Peter is that when asked about their drug use and the experiences they had during that time they both talk about it in a very positive way. Both held down jobs and neither experienced any significant negative health effects. As for the friends that Nicole has warned Hannah about, when I asked about them she admitted that she made them up. Her justification for this was that she wanted to scare Hannah and if she had told her the truth it would have made the drug too attractive.

Nicole and Peter are not alone in this type of major turnaround. There are many parents who did experiment and had 'positive' drug experiences but, when they have children of their own, their memories of their own drug use fade and they become very 'anti-drug'. My concern is what would happen if Hannah ever found out the truth about her parents' past? The breakdown of trust here could be devastating for this close-knit family.

Jim is almost 50 years old. He has been married to Sylvia for almost seventeen years and has two teenage daughters, Victoria and Maddie. Jim is a successful accountant and has been a regular cannabis user since his early twenties, and he drinks at least one bottle of wine every evening. He admits that he has a cannabis problem. He has tried to stop using many times over the years, succeeding for a period of time when his first daughter was born, but relapsing a number of years later. Since then, he has never been able to go for longer than a couple of days without using. He is also concerned about his alcohol consumption, although this is very much secondary to his concerns regarding his cannabis use and the effect that this may have on his relationship with his children.

He has never smoked in front of his daughters, who are now fourteen and sixteen years old, although both of them are aware of his drug use. When it comes to talking about drugs, Jim is completely honest. He and his wife began talking about drugs, and Jim's alcohol and drug use in particular, when the girls were in their early teens.

'We wanted to be as honest as we could,' said Jim. 'I have had both positive and negative experiences associated with my drug use and I've always told the girls that this is the story with most people. Giving my girls the whole story, warts and all, will hopefully help them to make good healthy choices. I wish I had made better choices when I was younger—no one ever gave me that option.'

Sixteen-year-old Victoria is extremely well informed about alcohol and drugs.

'Dad has used a pile of drugs over the years and he still uses dope,' she told me. 'I really wish he didn't but he has a problem. It doesn't really affect Maddie and me—he never smokes in front of us and only smokes very late at night. It used to be after we had gone to bed but now that we're older it's becoming harder for him to hide it. I hope he does finally find a way to stop.

'I'm really glad that we've been told everything. I have no interest in ever trying drugs—the struggles that Dad has had in trying to stop using and how embarrassed he is about the fact that he finds it so difficult to stop really don't make it too attractive to me. Dad has always said that smoking dope was fun when he was young but over a period of time the fun started to disappear and the problems increased. When you talk to Dad now about drugs, you can see that he gets no fun at all from it.

'By far the best thing about being able to talk about drugs so openly in our house has been being able to help friends at school. People talk about drugs a lot at school and so much of what people say, even the teachers, is just crap. I can come home, ask Mum or Dad, and get real answers.'

What a different approach and what a different outcome. Jim's honesty about his drug use has resulted in an extremely positive relationship with his children when it comes to drug information. We have no way of knowing the impact that having a drug-using parent will have on Victoria and Maddie in the long term, but currently they both have a very mature attitude towards drugs and the problems they can cause.

Jenny is a 40-year-old divorced mother of four. Like the vast majority of Australians she never used illicit drugs when she was younger and only drinks alcohol on special occasions. Two of her children, Jonathan and Nick, are in their mid-teens, and both have asked their mother whether she ever used drugs.

Due to the choices she made when she was younger she is able to answer them honestly and say that illegal drugs have never been a part of her life. However, according to Jenny there is a downside to her lack of experience.

'I know nothing about drugs,' said Jenny. 'My kids all know that I didn't take drugs when I was younger and I'm sure that makes what I say a little less credible. I do raise the issue of drugs with the boys, but if they ever asked me a question I really wouldn't have a clue what to say. I was one of those people that never even saw a drug when I was growing up, let alone took one. I do feel pretty ignorant.'

She attends any drug education sessions that her children's schools run and she tries to keep abreast of what is going on by watching documentaries and talking to people who she believes are better informed than she is. Jenny has made it very clear to her children that they can come to her no matter what—drugs are far from a taboo subject in their home—but according to Jenny none of her children have ever really taken up the opportunity to talk to her about the controversial subject. Every conversation about drugs that has taken place has been initiated by her.

'I'm pretty sure neither of the two older boys has ever used illegal drugs. Jonathan drinks alcohol and we've had a couple of issues with him coming home drunk after a big night. Although I don't want them to drink or take drugs, all of the kids know that no matter what they do, no matter what problem they find themselves in, they are still my boys and I love them. I hope they would come to me no matter what they have done.'

Jonathan has used cannabis. He experimented with the drug once or twice and didn't enjoy it, and as a result doesn't plan to use again. He has had a couple of nasty experiences with alcohol and both times have resulted in long discussions with his mother about the risks involved in excessive drinking.

'I would never talk to Mum about the fact I smoked weed,' the sixteen-year-old said. 'It's not that she would get angry or anything, I just know that it would disappoint her and I've heard her tell so many people that she "knows her boys don't use drugs" that I think it would embarrass her. I don't want to make her look like a liar.

'It is so obvious that Mum never took drugs. Some of the things that she says are so old-fashioned and that makes it really difficult to take a lot of what she says seriously. I have to say, though, that if one of my friends got into difficulty after taking drugs or got into trouble after drinking too much, I would call Mum. None of my other friends would say that, I'm sure—but Mum would be there for me and my friends, and she wouldn't judge. That's pretty unusual for a parent.'

These three examples of how parents have dealt with this confronting question illustrates that there are no easy answers. However, it seems to me that honesty is the best policy. Now this doesn't mean that you should be ramming the fact that you once had a puff of a joint in 1983 down your children's throat. However, if you're asked a direct question by your child, I believe that you should answer it truthfully.

We know that by far one of the most important elements of a positive parent–child relationship is honesty and trust. When you ask your child a question about something they have done, you would like them to answer honestly. Doesn't your child deserve the same respect?

So if you have used drugs, what should you say? To my mind the most important thing to focus on in your answer is why you *stopped* using. The reasons you give to your teenager about why you stopped are so important and say so much about the 'real' risks associated with drug use. It's also a candid and direct approach and young people really appreciate that. Some of the reasons that parents have given to their children for stopping include the following:

- 'I used cannabis once or twice and it just made me feel really sick. Some of my friends really liked it but it just wasn't me—I didn't enjoy smoking and I made the decision not to do it again.'
- 'Some of the people I was hanging out with used ecstasy and I decided to use it one night. I found the feeling really overpowering and very scary. It cost me $50 and I realised that I could spend that money on other things and not feel ill.'
- 'Cannabis was a big part of my life for a couple of years. I used almost every week until I finally realised that I wasn't doing anything else. I only hung out with cannabis users and I lost contact with other friends. Although it was fun at the beginning it certainly wasn't at the end.'
- 'Drugs can be fun. I certainly had a good time for a while but the bad experiences started to outweigh the good and I just got bored with the whole thing.'
- 'I stopped smoking when a very close friend of mine got busted. He got caught smoking a bong in a park and found himself at a police station. It wasn't until that happened that I really

understood that cannabis was illegal and you could get into serious trouble if you got caught. It just wasn't worth the risk.'

- 'I stopped using when I met your mum. She thought drugs were for losers and forced me to make a decision—it was her or the dope. I chose your mum!'

Whatever you decide to say to your child, try to avoid using the old chestnut 'I did try drugs but things are different now'. This is a cop-out and not based on any real evidence. It's a response that parents are increasingly using when it comes to cannabis in particular—'I did try cannabis but it's a lot stronger now'—and, as discussed on pages 118–121, is based on very poor evidence. It is a really weak response that teenagers see through pretty quickly and usually reject.

All parents want an honest and open relationship with their child. If, God forbid, something should go wrong and a child needs help with a drug and alcohol problem, every parent hopes that they are the first port of call when it comes to help and advice. However, if you're not honest with them, why on earth would they ever be honest with you?

• If I find drugs in my child's room, can I get them tested? Could I be prosecuted for having illegal drugs on my property?

This must be every parent's worst fear. No matter what your attitude towards drugs, I have yet to meet a parent who would be happy to discover that their child was experimenting in some way. When it comes to actually finding drugs in your child's room, it is likely to be the result of one of two scenarios.

The first of these involves a parent innocently putting their child's clothes away, or cleaning out their school bag, and accidentally finding a suspicious substance or some paraphernalia. For most parents it is usually a small plastic bag of cannabis or a bong or pipe. Recently, as ecstasy and amphetamines have become more popular, more and more parents who find themselves in this situation have come across a pill or a bag full of powder or fine crystals.

The second scenario is usually preceded by a period of suspicion and unrest in the family home. For whatever reason, the parents suspect that their child could be using drugs and they feel the need to find out whether or not their suspicions are correct. They then go through their teenager's room and possessions. If they actually find drugs, they are in the unenviable position of not only having to tell their child they found something, but also informing them that they have searched their room.

Neither of these situations is easy to deal with and both come with their own set of unique issues. Let's deal with the easier one first.

Accidentally discovering an illegal drug in your child's room is going to be a tremendous shock for any parent. No matter how you may have prepared yourself for such a discovery (and to be quite honest, I doubt whether any parent spends too long thinking about such a possibility), it is always going to evoke emotions like disappointment, anger and fear. Many parents will try to come up with some possible explanation for its presence, apart from the obvious.

The most important response is also the most difficult—don't overreact! Take some time to think through what you are going to do. Talk to your partner and discuss where, when and how you are going to raise the issue. Those three elements (the where, when and how) are all equally important and will play a major part in the success of your strategy.

At this stage, some parents become obsessed with wanting to know what it is that they have found. I have had many parents contact me over the years to ask if I know of anywhere that would test the substance. What surprises me is that so many of these mums and dads have not really thought through what they are considering doing. If it is an illegal drug, and they are caught in possession of it, there is every likelihood that they could be prosecuted. If they did take the drug somewhere for testing and it was found to be a drug like cannabis or ecstasy, the testing company would be legally bound to inform the police.

So how important is it to know what the drug is? For many parents it is imperative, particularly when it comes to pills and powders. If you find a bag of what looks like lawn clippings, you can pretty well bet that you've discovered cannabis. Pills could be pharmaceutical products (although most of those actually have names stamped onto them, or indentations designed to make them easier to break into halves or quarters—something you rarely see on illicit drugs like ecstasy) or illicits such as speed or ecstasy. Powders are usually the most concerning for parents as these could be anything from amphetamines to cocaine or even heroin.

Even though you may be desperate to get the substance tested, it is important that you drop the idea pretty quickly. In my experience, where parents have gone to the lengths of contacting police, they are usually told in no uncertain terms to flush the substance down the toilet and forget about testing due to the legal problems it will cause.

Your best bet of finding out what the substance is comes when you sit down and talk to your child about your discovery. If you have planned the discussion well and don't overreact, you might find that they are more willing to be honest and open with you. There are no hard and fast rules when it comes to discussions like this but there are four key elements that should assist in making it more successful:

- *Show your concern.* Make it clear you love your child unconditionally and nothing will change that. However, if they have been using illegal drugs they have broken the law and there will be consequences.
- *Choose your moment.* Make sure that you are calm and that your teenager is in the right headspace. Trying to have a conversation like this as soon as they walk through the door after school may not be the best time. You're also going to get a much better outcome if the discussion does not feel like an ambush.

- *Recognise problems.* The most important question you can ask your child is 'Why are you taking the drug?' If they say it gives them a good feeling or to have fun times with their friends, it is much more encouraging than if they start talking about using it to satisfy a need, to feel better or to solve problems.
- *Don't blame yourself.* Don't go down the road of thinking that you have failed as a parent. This is going to help no one and will only cause problems between you and your child.

When you first tell your child that you have discovered something in their room, one of the first questions you need to ask is 'What is it?' I hope that you get an answer, but over the years I have met many parents who have never been able to find out exactly what it was they found on that day. Often the teenager refuses to acknowledge that the drugs were theirs and pleads ignorance, and I am sure there have been times when young people have found themselves in situations where they truly have no idea where the drugs came from. In these instances you may never get an answer, but there still need to be consequences. If your child had been caught with those drugs in their possession by a police officer ignorance would be no defence. The same needs to apply in the home.

Bringing illicit drugs into the family home is an incredibly irresponsible thing to do and your child needs to realise what could have happened if the police had discovered the drugs before you did. One of the most important things that you should do after you have confronted your child with what you have found is to destroy the drugs (flushing them down the toilet is probably the best option), making it very clear to them that even your keeping them on the property since the discovery has put you at great risk of possible prosecution.

Being caught with illicit drugs by your parent is almost as confronting for the adolescent. You may well have felt disappointment and anger, but they are going to experience a great deal of shame. The fear of disappointing and letting down their parents is very real and, although it may seem that they don't care what you think of them at this stage of development, we know that they still do very much.

If there is a silver lining to this type of incident, it's going to be that a dialogue has started. Unfortunately, some parents never start talking to their children about drugs until something like this happens. If they get their response right and don't overreact there is the possibility that some good may come out of it.

When the discovery of drugs is the result of a search through the child's possessions because of a belief that something is amiss, the result is usually quite different and rarely ends positively.

Lynette had always promised herself that she wouldn't become a mother who spied on her child, but as her daughter got older, circumstances changed and she became worried about her behaviour.

Jacinta was a year twelve student who had a great circle of friends. However, over a short period of time Jacinta seemed to lose touch with many of her old group. She became much more secretive about who she was hanging out with and when her parents asked her anything about what she was doing and where she was going it usually ended in a fight. Lynette tried to address her concerns with her daughter but it landed on deaf ears.

One day, when Jacinta was at school and Lynette was putting some of her clothes away, she went through her things. According to Lynette, she hadn't planned to do it but she was worried and she needed to find out what was happening. She had no idea what she was looking for but searched anyway.

'At the bottom of one of her drawers I found a small plastic bag with two small pink pills in it. Each of the pills had a crescent moon on it. I had no idea what to do and how to ask her about what I had found.'

One of the major problems Lynette was grappling with was that she had abused her daughter's trust and, even though she had discovered ecstasy in her daughter's room, the means didn't seem to justify the ends. She had become the mother she had never wanted to be!

I suppose you have to ask the question—did she have any other option?

It would seem that Lynette had tried all other avenues. She had attempted to have a conversation with her daughter about her concerns many times—all had failed. It seemed that there was no other choice but to search the room.

The fallout from the discovery was immense and the reason Lynette contacted me was because she was trying to find a counsellor who could help her mend the damaged mother–daughter relationship. Jacinta had left home and would not communicate with her mother at all. It would appear as though all trust in the relationship had been broken. Not only had Lynette been through her daughter's room, leading to her daughter feeling betrayed, Jacinta had been using drugs, totally destroying the trust her mother had in her. It had become a terrible situation which was going to be incredibly difficult to resolve.

Searching your child's room, sending the youngster off to be drug tested or purchasing products that can detect traces of drugs on your child's possessions are all extreme responses to the possibility that your child could be using drugs. Unfortunately, there are some parents, like Lynette, who find themselves in situations where they feel they have no other choice.

The one thing you don't want to lose with your child is trust. Of course, if you feel that your adolescent is in danger you may have no other option, but make sure that you have tried all other avenues and that you fully understand the implications of such a strategy.

• A lot of famous people talk about their drug use and they don't seem to have had any major problems. Are drugs really as bad as they are made out to be?

In recent times more and more celebrities have either been caught using drugs or have decided to write a 'tell-all' autobiography and spill the beans about their past drug use. Those who have willingly decided to share their past drug experiences, often for large amounts of money, usually tell about the 'horrors' of the days they used drugs and the downward spiral they found themselves in once they began. For those who get caught in compromising situations with drugs, there are usually heartfelt apologies for their behaviour and sometimes bizarre explanations for the choices they have made.

The media have also become increasingly interested in celebrity drug use, often asking people direct questions about whether they have ever experimented with substances. Even politicians have not escaped this trend, particularly in regard to cannabis.

The major problem is the message that these admissions send to young people. Although many would imagine that stories of famous people using drugs and experiencing a range of problems would discourage teenagers from going down the same path, in many cases just the opposite happens. You'd think that hearing a rock star like Keith Richards talk about his drug use and then taking a look at him would be enough to put anyone off ever touching illicit substances! Unfortunately the only message that some young people pick up is that these celebrities have 'made it through to the other side' and continue to lead very glamorous and successful lives.

When you look at the messages that we give young people about drugs they are usually negative, warning about the risks associated with their use. Drugs destroy lives—people who use them lose their jobs, their families and are very unhealthy. This just doesn't match what they see when the latest rock star tells all on a TV chat show, or a famous sportsman has been caught doing the 'wrong thing'. Even if they did have a bad time there for a while, they certainly don't look like they're suffering too much at the moment. These cases also cause young people to question the legal issues around drug use when they see celebrities who are caught with illicit substances getting off with a slap on the wrist.

In recent years a number of high-profile sportsmen have been caught using a range of illegal drugs, and for the most part these are the celebrities that usually get brought up in classroom discussions, particularly by young men. How can you really answer a question about the harms associated with drug use when incredibly successful men in peak physical condition admit to regular drug use?

Mixed messages are extremely dangerous when it comes to providing drug information to young people. Celebrity drug use, particularly the way it is represented in the media, often contradicts everything they are taught by everyone else. This is why it is incredibly important that we don't present drug information in a black and white way. There are no definites when it comes to the effects any drug will have on a person. When we talk to young people we need to make sure that we discuss the range of effects of drugs, not just the possibility of death. There are physical, psychological and, importantly, social effects that can arise as a result of using alcohol and other drugs. In some cases, the use of drugs may not result in any major physical effects that anyone can see, but the mental health repercussions may be immense. In other cases, the physical impacts of long-term drug use may be obvious.

The social impacts of drug use are not discussed often enough but are very real and can have devastating effects. When it comes to sportsmen, for example, the use of illicit drugs can lead to a change in how others in the community regard them. A footballer who is found to be using a drug like ecstasy can find his reputation is damaged for the rest of his life. He could win every award possible in his future career in the sport, but I guarantee he will always be known as 'the footballer who took ecstasy'. The impact on his family and friends can also be devastating and is rarely talked about.

Celebrity drug use does cause significant problems for educators and parents, who are struggling to work out how they handle questions about this new phenomenon. Incredibly successful people (who are usually also beautiful, thin and extremely rich!) being caught or admitting to drug use, with little or no signs of adverse effects, challenge the messages we are trying to deliver. That is why we have to get the message right.

Making sure the information we give young people is balanced, accurate and credible is crucial. Acknowledging that not everyone is going to experience the same problems will enable us to explain why some people appear to get by unscathed. At the same time, no matter who you are, there are problems—some you may not be able to observe by watching the nightly news, but they are there.

• Does all drug use lead to addiction?

When a parent discovers that their child has used any drug, one of the first thoughts that enters their mind is that this could be the beginning of the slippery slope to addiction. This is a completely understandable fear, as most of the information that we receive about drugs focuses on the 'hard end' of the market and people who have experienced significant problems with their drug use. Although there are those people who lump all drug use into the same barrel the reality is somewhat different. As discussed in Chapter 1, there are five types of drug use and people may move in and out of these at different stages in their lives.

Not surprisingly, the most problematic type of drug use is the one most likely to be represented in the media—*dependent or compulsive use*. This describes a situation where a person uses a drug regularly for so long that the drug-induced state feels normal to them and they feel compelled to use the drug in everyday life, even though it could be causing them great problems.

Not all drug users are dependent on their drug of choice. Although it is not something we usually talk about, the simple fact of the matter is that many people who experiment with drugs do so for a short period of time and come out the other end relatively unscathed. Unfortunately, some do not.

No, not all drug use leads to addiction. However, all drug use—whether it be legal, illegal or pharmaceutical—is risky and it is important that anyone considering using any drug is aware of all of the possible risks.

AFTERWORD

The information in this book has been provided to assist families to have a positive dialogue about alcohol and other drugs. Pretty much every parent knows that it is important to talk to their kids about drugs, but deciding *what* to actually talk about (and how to bring it up) can be extremely difficult. Some of the questions in this book are simply conversation starters for you and your children; others give background information for you as a parent to help you work out how to deal with a particular issue should it arise. I hope you have found these suggestions useful.

Last week I was invited to speak to a school community (the students, staff and parents) about alcohol and young people. The day went extremely well. When I finished speaking to the student groups, I asked one of the teachers about the larger school drug-education program and where my presentation fitted into the overall philosophy of the school. His answer really had an impact on me and illustrated why I had had such a wonderful response from the students throughout the day.

'Drug education is a process at our school, not an event,' he said quite simply.

Let's look closely at this statement: in particular, what does it mean for families dealing with this complex subject?

Too often I get asked to go to a school and give a one hour talk to a group of students and then walk away. The idea is to bring in an outside speaker who has some expertise in the area to give a presentation about the topic, and then the teacher can tick the box and say that they have covered the drug issue. Drug education becomes an 'event'.

Unfortunately this can happen in the home as well. Discussions around alcohol and other drugs often arise only when an incident occurs. They are reactive, usually involve warnings and threats of punishment, and hardly ever end up well for either the parent or the child. If parents could try to make drug education more of a 'process', with regular positive conversations where your children are informed of your views and opinions on alcohol and drugs, perhaps there would be a better chance of more healthy and successful outcomes.

INDEX